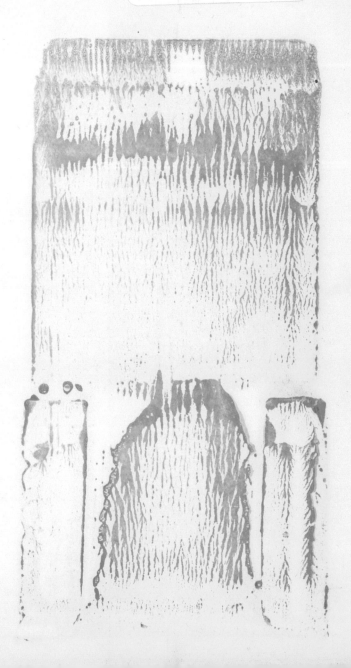

SOUTH ARABIA

South Arabia
Arena of Conflict

TOM LITTLE

FREDERICK A. PRAEGER, *Publishers*
New York · Washington · London

FREDERICK A. PRAEGER, *Publishers*
111 Fourth Avenue, New York, N.Y. 10003, U.S.A.
77-79 Charlotte Street, London W.1, England

Published in the United States of America in 1968
by Frederick A. Praeger, Inc., Publishers

© 1968 in London, England, by Tom Little

Library of Congress Catalog Card Number: 68-19644

Printed in Great Britain

Contents

To Vera

Preface

THE NEW STATE in South Arabia was named the People's Republic of South Yemen only in the last days before independence on November 30, 1967, but this was of small importance beside the fact that the territories it would include were uncertain even three months earlier. Even if all had been known when work started on this book, it could not have notably changed the contents. The contrapuntal character of the relationship of South Arabia and Yemen, the names used by the militant nationalist parties, the continuing hope for the political unity of the whole area—all made it necessary to include an account of Yemen even though it was already well-established as a separate state.

South Arabia has been an arena of conflict and may well remain so for a long time to come, but one must hope that the Arabs will learn to go their own way in peace. Their intelligence and many skills will avail them little unless they acquire quickly the tolerance required to live together.

There was certainly little tolerance between Arab and Arab in the final years of struggle. The two militant parties—FLOSY and the NLF—stood for exactly the same thing and the British offered them everything they wanted before the end, but there was no halt to the fighting until one party emerged the victor. It was a victory costly to the country, and part of the price may yet have to be paid in feuds and enmities. If this result seems totally unreasonable, it must be judged beside the events which led up to it.

This book sets out to tell the story from the beginning, before the dust of conflict has settled or the passage of time given perspective to it. No doubt there will be much argument in Britain about who was to blame for the failure to construct a neat and peaceful federation or unitary state. I am inclined to think that, if the concept was capable of consummation in the fifties, it had already ceased to be so in the sixties, and that all who worked upon it then were trying to perform the impossible. Perhaps the painful birth of the republic gives cause to ask whether it is ever wise to impose alien political patterns on an unsophisticated people.

Because events in Yemen have affected South Arabia so much, I have interspersed sections about Yemen as closely as possible to the periods of South Arabian history they most concerned. I may have given too much detail about the merger of Aden with the Federation of the Amirates of the South. If so, I can only say that I think it was the crucial turning-point, when all the difficulties to come were manifest.

I have kept the maps to the simplest of outlines and have not included the boundaries of the former Protectorate states because they are meaningless except on a very much larger scale.

I should like to thank Mrs Peggy Ball of Whitchurch-on-Thames for typing most of the manuscript, Mr I. H. Elfick of Pangbourne Nautical College for help with the maps of the Federation and the Republic and Mrs S. A. Dallas, also of Whitchurch, for the map of Aden.

In conclusion, I must pay tribute to my Pakistani colleague, Ibrahim Noori, the Regional News Service and Reuter correspondent, who bore the brunt of a difficult and often dangerous assignment for over five years. He gave me help, guidance and protection on my visits to Aden; but I must put on record that he did not see the text of this book before it was in print, and he is in no way responsible for my opinions or forms of expression.

Tom Little

Whitchurch-on-Thames,
Oxon.
December 10, 1967.

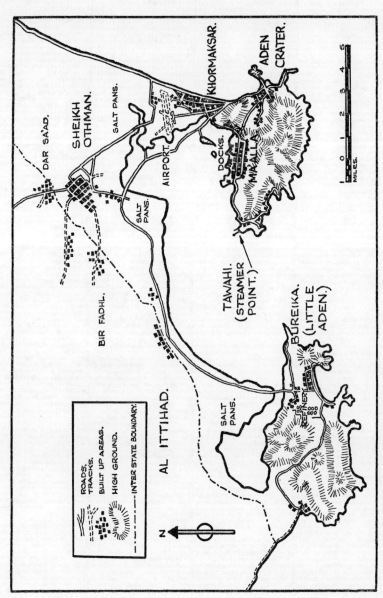

I. ADEN: *Area of former Aden Colony*

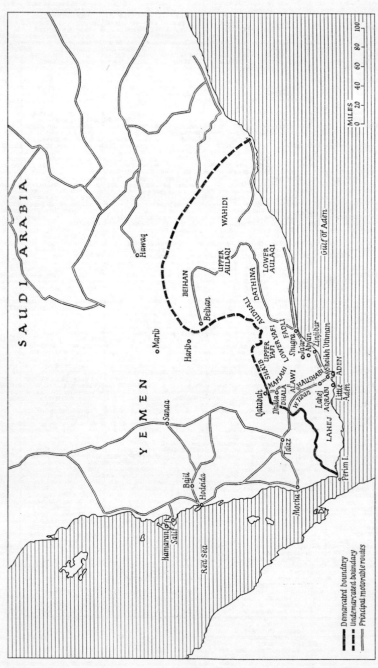

II. *Federation of South Arabia*

SAUDI ARABIA

YEMEN

Red Sea

Gulf of Aden

Sanaa
Marib
Hawaq
Hodeida
Bajil
Taizz
Mocha
Kamaran I.
Salif
Perim I.
Harib
Beihan
BEIHAN
WAHIDI
UPPER AULAQI
LOWER AULAQI
DATHINA
AUDHALI
Qataba
SHAIB
UPPER YAFI
MAFLAHI
LOWER YAFI
DHALA
Dhala
FADLI
Shuqra
Abyan
Zinjibar
Jaar
Sheikh Uthman
ALAWI
HAUSHAB
w'Ruwan
Lahej
AQRABI
LAHEJ
Little Aden
ADEN

MILES
0 20 40 60 80 100

Demarcated boundary
Undemarcated boundary
Principal motorable routes

x

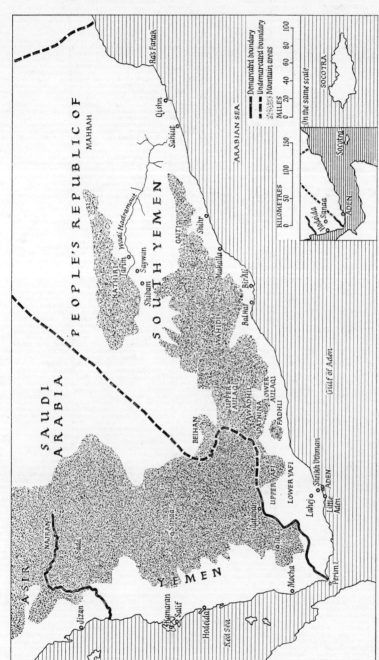

III. People's Republic of South Yemen

xi

I

Ancient Kingdoms and the Inheritors

SOUTH ARABIA was always only a vague geographical description until it was given a political meaning in very recent years. It is a region of barren mountain and desert clinging to the south-western tip of the Arabian peninsula between the 10th and 15th Parallels, but its frontiers are disputed and even its name is claimed for larger territories that include it. Its borders are hardly anywhere determined by natural features and its people are part of wider and complex tribal groups.

The peninsula is a platform of crystalline rock overlaid with sandstone sediments which is tilted downwards from the west to the east. On the higher western edge the upsurge of molten rock from beneath the earth's crust through fractures in the platform has produced higher plateaux with frequent volcanic cones usually over 8,000 feet in height and sometimes reaching 10,000 feet. Although water in ancient times cut deep valleys in the platform, there are now no perennial rivers flowing down its slopes. Yemen and South Arabia are part of the configuration. The highest mountain in the entire peninsula is Bani Shaib in Yemen, about 14,000 feet in height. Both countries consist of mountains, plateaux and ravines, and not a single river rising in the highlands flows all the year or successfully traverses the coastal plains to the sea.

I

This pitiful land was once part of a thriving tribal empire whose origins are lost in antiquity. The Minaean people established their dominance over the tribes in an area roughly corresponding to southeast Yemen and the Hadramaut in an indeterminate period of Arabian pre-history. They are known to have had kings ruling over a state-like structure in the fourteenth century B C and to have had trade connections with Egypt at the time; but even earlier they, or people like them, had associations with the Babylonian and other Middle Eastern peoples. The royal residence was at Qarnaw, which is the present-day village of Ma'in, near Sanaa in Yemen. They worshipped an astral trinity consisting of the Moon God, the principal deity responsible for the safety of the state, the Sun Goddess, and Venus, first of the stars who were their offspring.

The wealth of the Minaean kingdom derived from a bush, or small tree with many stems, which exuded a fragrant resin through cuts made in its bark. This was frankincense, found nowhere else in the world. The resin hardened in the sun and was carried by camel caravans across Arabia or shipped from Aden and other south coast ports for the sacrificial fires of Egypt, Babylon, Persia and Greece. In this way began one of the oldest of caravan roads, the Incense Route, by which the frankincense, myrrh and spices of South Arabia, and the products of China and India unshipped at the coast, reached Mesopotamia and the Mediterranean. To protect it the Minaeans built forty strongholds of cut-stone about 20 feet high and 12 feet thick, reaching from Maan in Jordan to the valley of the lower Euphrates.

The Minaeans eventually fell to an enemy within the gates, a primitive desert people further north who bred the camels for the caravans and protected them on their journeys through Arabia. They became known as the Sabaeans, that is, of Saba: the Sheba of the Book of Job. These hardy tribesmen abandoned their desert homelands to settle in the fertile valleys of Yemen and the Hadramaut during the ninth and tenth centuries B C, becoming at first the partners and then the masters of the Minaeans.

The Sabaeans built up a powerful confederation of tribes, each under its own chieftain and responsible for the cultivation of frankincense, the irrigation of its fields and the protection of travellers through its territory. For about 300 years the paramount ruler of the confederation was a priest-king living at what is now the village of Kharibah, east of Sanaa in Yemen, but about 650 BC there was a change within the Sabaean polity and the ruler moved to Marib, about sixty miles east of Sanaa, and became a secular king.

This kingdom of Saba was the first state of South Arabia, but its power reached far beyond its frontiers, to Petra and the Euphrates. No one could challenge its control of the trade in frankincense, myrrh and spices, in the fabrics, the ivory, the precious stones and the gold of Africa and India, which they sold to Egypt, Babylonia and Assyria and to the Phoenicians who carried them far away beyond the confines of their known world. The starting point of the Sabaean Incense Route is believed to have been at Husn al-Ghurab, a tiny rock-island about 200 miles east of Aden. From the shores of the Hadramaut, the route passed by several tracks skirting the forests of frankincense trees further inland to converge on Shabwa. From there it continued north to Petra, where it divided into three roads, the first traversing the Sinai into Egypt, the second continuing north to Jerusalem, Damascus, Tyre and Sidon, and the third passing eastward to Nineveh in Mesopotamia.

The Sabaeans created an elaborate system of roads and tracks with warehouses at key points and fortified watchtowers to protect the trade. These were established and maintained by a political and administrative organisation that was highly sophisticated by the standards of the times. The kingdom was therefore the first approximation to an Arabian state, in the proper sense, in that it was the first to possess a central organisation. The commercial centre at Shabwa may have been the royal city of the Queen of Sheba, for it was there that the royal residence of the Sabaeans was established, but the capital was at Marib which had natural defences in the volcanic group of peaks surrounding it and was further fortified by human art.

The dam at Marib bore witness to the strength of the central organisation. It was first constructed in Minaean times to control the Dhana river in Wadi Saba (the present-day Wadi al-Sadd or 'Valley of the Dam') to irrigate the cultivable land and to protect the city from periodic flooding. It resembled in a primitive way the modern rock-fill dams, of which the High Dam at Aswan is a late example, consisting of earth banked and sloped towards the oncoming river, covered with small stones with such skill that the surface was impermeable, and rooted in large rocks at each end. Slabs of limestone formed sluice gates that released the irrigation water through channels running under the dam, while the unwanted surplus by-passed it through a diversion channel or waterfall. This dam, about a third of a mile in length, was the basis of the domestic agricultural wealth of the ancient kingdoms. Its collapse marked the end of an era and has been celebrated in several Arabian legends, but it is not known whether an earthquake destroyed it or whether it was the victim of the internal strife that was ruining the kingdom.

In its late period, the Sabaean kingdom depended for its strength on a military caste, which was something like a professional army. This caste was drawn (possibly to prevent its mastering the kingdom) from two rival tribes, the Himyar and the Hamdan. In time, however, they challenged the Sabaeans as well as each other, and in 115 BC the kingdom fell apart into its natural geographical divisions: the coastal region of the Hamdan tribe, and the Himyarite area of high land based on Shabwa. Thus began the Himyarite period which endured until early in the sixth century AD and which, at the height of its power, extended deep into the Arabian desert and reached the shores of the Persian Gulf.

A mound of ruins on the road from Sanaa to Mecca marks the site of the Himyarites' first capital at Zaphar; but, as they overcame the Hamdan in a century-and-a-half of struggle, they moved their royal centre to Sanaa. The wealth of the kingdom was already beginning to decline with the breaking of the Arabian commercial monopoly by the development of new routes to carry the Indian trade through Mesopotamia, and by Roman ships plying in the Persian Gulf and the Indian Ocean. Neglect of irrigation and the collapse of the Marib Dam completed the impoverishment of the country.

There is evidence that this decline took place over a long period in which people drifted away from the towns and countryside. Some of them emigrated to Abyssinia, a Christian kingdom, and perhaps this stimulated Abyssinian efforts to conquer the Himyarites. Christianity and Judaism had already entered South Arabia. Jewish colonies began to establish themselves after the fall of Jerusalem in AD 70, and the last of the Himyarite rulers, Dhu Naawas, was a Jew.* The first Christian mission to South Arabia was sent by the Emperor Constantius II in 356; it was led by a monk called Theophilus Indus, who built a church in Aden, one of the earliest in South Arabia. The main centre of the Christians was in the region of what is now the Saudi Arabian town of Najran, lying just over the border from Yemen. But the attempts of Abyssinia to invade the country brought the Christians into disrepute. In revenge for the persecution of the Christians by Dhu Naawas, the Abyssinian Emperor mounted his biggest offensive and overthrew him in 525 AD. This was the end of Himyarite power, but the Christian triumph was short-lived. Fifty years later, the Persians seized the kingdom, and little more than half a century afterwards South Arabia embraced Islam and slowly but surely was absorbed by the empire of the Caliphs.

II

There was never any greatness again in South Arabia. No power controlled the tribes. Under the Himyarites, even more than under the Sabaeans, they had enjoyed local autonomy under their own leaders; and under the Abyssinians, the Persians and the caliphate they were independent within the flimsiest authority. They lived in anarchy, modified only by tribal custom and the most primitive of religious law.

The fame of the ancient kingdoms survives in legend, in names, in heaps of stones and sometimes in customs. The Banu Ma'in tribes of Yemen still meet in the Grand Council of Ma'in: a tribal institution that has lived through the centuries since Minaean times. The stones of the Marib Dam are built into the houses of the village of Marib; and in Aden there is a family called Luqman whose name goes back to Luqman ibn Ad, the mythical king reputed to have built the dam. The Banu Yafai tribes of South Arabia probably

---

*The Prophet Mohammed may have acquired his knowledge of Jewish and Christian scriptures on the Arabian caravan routes.

B

take their name from Yafa, the Sabaean deity, and in Yemen there are the Banu Saba and the Banu Hamdan, descendants of the enemies of the Himyar. Frankincense is still an export from Aden selling at about £60 a ton. Until 1948, when about 15,000 Jews departed for Israel, South Arabia had a strong Jewish community dating from the fall of Jerusalem in the first century AD.

The Muttawakkilite Imams of Yemen claim descent from the Himyarite kings. They keep this claim alive 'by sprinkling red powder on their signature'.* Whatever may be the evidence of this family descent, it is beyond question that Yemen was for centuries in early times the cornerstone of a powerful tribal confederation and that for long periods it was dominant far beyond its borders. When the Romans (following the Greek usage) spoke of *Arabia Felix*, they did not mean Yemen as it is today but the entire western spine of the peninsula from Aden to its point of disappearance in the Nefud desert to the north. Although the term recognised a geographical more than a political pattern, it reflected the fact that Yemen's history was an inextricable part of the history of the Minaeans, the Sabaeans and the Himyarites. Other strong tribal groups, such as the Abdali in South Arabia, were similarly submerged in the records of the kingdoms; but, whereas for centuries they were hardly identified, Yemen was. Its distinctive identity was a significant feature of early times, and has continued so to the present day.

The long period of time when they were a ruling people bred in the Yemenis an independence of mind and spirit which made them difficult to subdue either by the word or the sword, and to this day they are the largest unorthodox group of Muslims in the Arabian peninsula. Early in the mission of the Prophet Mohammed some Yemeni tribes declared their allegiance to him, but they soon turned to another prophet, Ayhaba, in protest against Mohammed's *zakat*, or poor tax. With their help Ayhaba made himself master of the country, and the Caliph Abu Bakr was compelled in 633 to send a force to secure his submission to the spiritual and secular authority

*Stephan and Nandy Ronart, *Concise Encyclopaedia of Arabic Civilisation* 1959. The word for red, *ahmar*, is present in the tribal name Himyar.

of the caliphate. The Yemenis nevertheless continued to do much what they liked in both religious and political affairs. Jewish, Christian and pagan communities existed long after Islamic tolerance began to wane, and the community established by Theophilus Indus even maintained its relations with Christianity outside the peninsula.

Three centuries after Abu Bakr's campaign against Ayhaba, revolutionary Qarmatians of the radical Ismailite Shia sect of Islam conquered the Tihamah, the coastal plain of Yemen. The Shia cult, however, was suppressed after a short period, and orthodox Sunni Islam was thus confirmed among the people of the plain. It failed to prevail over the highland people, however, for these were proselytised by the Imam of the unorthodox Zeidis, Yahya ibn Hussein al-Rassi, who in 897 arrived in the Sanaa area from Jabal al-Ras, near Medinah. The highland tribes were so sympathetic to his message that no amount of official opposition could prevent him from firmly planting his sect in the country. In course of time, the Zeidite faith was accepted by all the people of the highlands, and was preserved by them through centuries of orthodox rule. To this day it separates them from the orthodox Shafei people in the rest of South Arabia and is a factor of political importance.

South Arabia thenceforward was a rough and rebellious world, fallen far from the greatness of the ancient kingdoms. Although caught up by the strife within the caliphate, the changes of authority made little difference to it. The Fatimids ruled from Egypt for 150 years in the tenth and eleventh centuries and the Abbasids ruled from 1175 to 1250. After the Abbasid collapse, Yemen was left to itself until 1520, when it was incorporated into the Ottoman empire and put under the authority of a Turkish Pasha, governing from Sanaa. But even the Pasha of the Ports could do little to subdue the tribal and religious turbulence. In 1597, Al-Mansur Billah al-Qasim was elected Imam of the Zeidis and began a war of independence against the Turks which resulted in his gaining effective control of Yemen. He is regarded as the first in the direct line of descent of Yemeni Imams whose rule continued until 1962.

When the fanatically orthodox Wahabis swept across the Arabian desert early in the nineteenth century and invaded Yemen, they succeeded in carrying away both the unorthodox Imam and the Turkish Pasha, but they had no more success than previous upholders of orthodox doctrine in converting the Yemeni highlanders. Ibrahim Pasha, soldier-son of Mohammed Ali of Egypt, was sent at the Sultan's request to subdue the Wahabis, and in 1818 he drove them out of Yemen. With more political wisdom than religious conviction, Ibrahim restored the Zeidi Imams, carefully leaving his garrison troops in the Shafei ports of Hodeida, Zabid and Mocha.

The Zeidis of Yemen showed little gratitude for the restoration of their Imam, and their rebelliousness to all authority, however nominal, kept the area in turmoil for most of the nineteenth century. They rose against Turco-Egyptian rule in 1836; this rebellion was crushed in the following year, and the Imam abdicated. But three years later, when Turkish troops and officials replaced the Egyptians in the plains, the Turks sought to conciliate the highlanders by according full sovereignty to the Imam in the interior of the country. In 1840, Sharif Hussein of Abu Arish conquered the Tihamah, which led to a war between him and the Imam nine years later. When the Turks sought to intervene, their expeditionary force was routed.

The Ottoman forces clung precariously to the coastal strip but were too wary to exploit the quarrels in the Muttawakkilite family. In the six years from 1850, there were no less than nine Imams, and strife reduced the highlands to anarchy. At last the Turks tired of their troublesome vassals and sent a powerful force into the hills in 1872, capturing Sanaa and ruthlessly subduing all resistance. This brought something that passed for peace for the rest of the century.

III

Until the middle of the last century, the harbour at Aden was situated in what is now known as Front Bay and Holkat Bay, on the eastern side of the rocky peninsula that shelters the almost enclosed water where the present port is sited. Although it is difficult to understand now why the more secure waters of the present port were ignored, it was certainly not because Aden was unimportant in the days of the ancient kingdoms. It was a centre for Minaean, Sabaean,

Himyarite, Egyptian, Phoenician, Greek and Roman trade, and was coveted in those times even as it was coveted hundreds of years later by European maritime powers. In the days of Constantine it had splendid fortifications and a flourishing commerce with all quarters of the known world.

With the decline of the Incense Route and the South Arabian tribes, Aden also declined, and in common with its hinterland it had little recorded history for a thousand years. From the tenth century, when it must have become nominally subject to the Imams of Yemen, the deepening poverty of the surrounding tribes reduced it to the status of a fishing village. Portents of the future came early in the sixteenth century, when Don Alphonso d'Albuquerque arrived from Goa with his Portuguese fleet and tried without success to storm the old fortifications. Another attempt at conquest was made by the Sultan of Egypt three years later. This also failed, but in 1538 the Turks seized the port by a variation of the Trojan Horse stratagem, landing a party of sick men who proved healthy enough to take the town from within. The Adenis soon grew tired of the Turks and in 1551 they handed the town over to the Portuguese. This first experiment in European rule was short-lived, however, for the Turks recovered Aden some months later and remained in possession. They made it a strongly fortified town, and this was how the English found it in 1609, when a ship of the East India Company first anchored there.

The object of the European maritime countries was to secure Aden as a safe base for their ships on their journeys to the East, and Dutch, Swedish, Danish and English merchants all sought to establish trading posts in the vicinity by peaceful means. All of these efforts were frustrated by the Ottoman Sultans, but so insignificant to their empire had the port become by the middle of the seventeenth century that the Turks withdrew. It was then neglected by everyone until the British, in the development of their sea power and Eastern trading empire, took possession of the port in 1839. All visible signs of Aden's past greatness had by that time disappeared and been replaced by squalid poverty. Only a century earlier there had still been the fine baths, with their domed roof and walls lined

9

with marble, and several excellent two-storey houses; but the decay then in evidence had continued through the years until a mere 500 people lived in hovels among the ruins.

The impecunious Sultans of Lahej used Aden as a base for their scarecrow pirates but in the early years of the century they usually left British ships alone. There was a reason for this favoured-nation treatment; in 1802 Britain had entered into its first commitment in South Arabia by signing a treaty of friendship and commerce with the Sultan of Lahej, Ahmed ibn Abdel Kerim. This treaty worked very well until Ahmed was succeeded in 1837 by his nephew, al-Muhasin, who proved hostile to Britain and broke the treaty in 1838. He little knew what he was doing. The British government was already concerned that Viceroy Mohammed Ali of Egypt was challenging the authority of his master the Sultan of Turkey and had demonstrated that he had an army competent enough in the field to develop ambitions of his own in Arabia. At the same time, the British recognised the potential importance of Aden to the India trade and therefore saw the necessity of keeping it free from interference by other powers and marauding Arabs from the desert. When the Sultan al-Muhasin's robbers raided a wrecked Indian ship flying the British flag and held the crew and passengers to ransom, this was taken as a pretext to seize the town.

Captain Haines, despatched by the Bombay Presidency with two warships mounting together 38 guns and carrying 700 troops, captured Aden in 1839 and annexed it to the British Crown, becoming the first British Resident there. He remade the treaty with Lahej three times by defeating the hostile Sultan in 1839, 1843 and 1844, but he had more success and less trouble with the Subeihi, Fadhli, Agrabi, Lower Yafai and Haushabi chieftains. The treaties he signed with these leaders were the nucleus of the system on which British protection was founded later in the century. Captain Haines himself had little personal luck in this enterprise, for on his return to India he was arraigned for corruption on complaints that later study suggests were founded on envy rather than fact, and he died in a most miserable condition in an Indian gaol. His name is nevertheless recorded in history as one of the empire-builders.

The sultanate of Lahej which gave Captain Haines so much trouble had had identity and importance during the ancient kingdoms when its people were one of the important tribes of the confederations that composed them. Early in the Islamic period the Omayyid Caliphs united it with Yemen. Later the Abbasids considered it part of a province extending from Mecca to Aden, but at the very outset of their rule the Caliph Mamoun granted Lahej autonomy under a family of hereditary governors, the Ziyadites, descendants of Abdullah ibn Ziyad. This family was ousted by the Banu Maan, whose territory consisted of that part of the Hadramaut as far as the town of Al-Shir. By uniting Lahej to Aden and their own lands, the Banu Maan effectively ruled an area roughly equivalent to the federal area of South Arabia proposed by the British in the 1960s.

This tribal prefiguration of a future state did not last long, for in 1728 Fadhl ibn Ali secured the independence of Lahej and seven years later conquered Aden. Fadhl was of the Abdali group of tribes which belonged to the area. He established the line which rules Lahej to this day, and it was his grandson, Sultan Ahmed ibn Abdel Kerim, who concluded the first treaty of friendship with the British in 1802.

Britain's emergence as the paramount maritime power at the end of the eighteenth century effectively brought Aden and its immediate hinterland out of the seclusion of a thousand years or more, for the raids and diplomatic skirmishing of the earlier European trading countries had barely touched it. The extensive confederation of tribes that constituted the Minaean, Sabaean and Himyarite kingdoms were only interesting historical foreshadowings of statehood in a fragmented and poverty-stricken region, whose harsh physical geography arrested all civilised development and material progress. This helps to explain why the British concept of a South Arabian state 120 years later gave rise to profound scepticism among those who knew the area. There was virtually no cohesion of peoples, for rule from Mecca, Damascus, Cairo and Constantinople had been so tenuous throughout the centuries that it hardly touched the tribal anarchy of the area, and when it did do so the change was always short-lived.

Yemen, as has been noted, preserved a degree of separate identity. This was partly due to nearly 300 years of total seclusion, from the end of the Ayyubid Islamic dynasty in the middle of the thirteenth century to its incorporation in the Ottoman empire early in the sixteenth. The oral traditions of Yemen's great antiquity when its rulers commanded a great part of Arabia from their capitals on the western edge of the peninsula, the legends of the Marib Dam, the ruins of royal cities and the strong walls of others, combined to engender in the people the belief that they had the right to rule the region. This belief was reflected in the claim of the Zeidi Imams to descent from the Himyarite kings. The coastal plain and the highlands were not always united, however, and in later times the power of the Imams seldom extended far beyond their ill-defined frontiers.

For about 170 years, between the successful revolt of Al-Mansur Billah al-Qasim (who achieved the independence of Yemen and founded the line of Zeidi Imams) and 1728, when the Sultan of Lahej ousted the Yemenis from Abdali territories, the Imam's sovereignty had some reality in South Arabia, but it was no more effective than that of the caliphates or the Ottoman empire. Nor was their supreme power within their own country continuous. They were conquered by the Wahabis, and though the Wahabis were in turn driven out by the Egyptians who re-established Ottoman authority, this last restored the Imams to rule only over the highlands. Even the Tihamah plain won its independence in the middle of the troubled nineteenth century. The Turks reconquered Sanaa in 1872, and the Zeidi rulers did not recover their country until the collapse of the Ottoman empire in 1918, despite the Imam Yahya's constant struggle to do so.

The Imams' refusal to accept Ottoman overlordship and their continuous rebellion against it established their claim to Yemen when Turkey was defeated in the First World War. Their claim to Aden and the tribal territories to the south-east, which were to become the South Arabian Federation, rested on the argument that the independence of peoples within the Ottoman empire left the region in their charge. This was by no means as strong as their claim to Yemen, but it had some foundation in the fact that a number of the tribal rulers traditionally received their investiture from the Imam of Yemen. Even so, the tradition of accepting investiture from the Imams was only a tactful avoidance of trouble with a country whose dominance was not feared. Among those who accepted investiture was the Sultan of Lahej, whose claim to independent possession of his small country dated from the successful rebellion of 1728 and was ever afterwards preserved, at first by the power of the Sultans themselves and then by an alliance with the British, except for a very brief period when the Turks re-established their authority after the British withdrew for a time in the 1914–18 war. Yemeni rule never existed in fact because the Imams were never in complete control of their own country, which was almost continuously in a state of civil war and sometimes in anarchy.

Tribal areas, even the kingdom of Yemen, do not have firm frontiers, although the grazing and the water of barren lands are demarcated by traditional rights that rarely change. People wander about, within and across them and establish a 'oneness' of living even when there is no unity over-riding tribal differences. It is this mixing of peoples of common descent, religion and language, rather than any legal claim, that gives some meaning to the concept of a state embracing all South Arabia.

2

Protection and Advice

WHEN THE BRITISH occupied Aden, they had no desire to commit themselves beyond the very narrow limits of protecting the port and securing what little trade there was to be had. This was true of most positions occupied by Britain during the nineteenth century, for public opinion there, at least until its close, was generally suspicious of all imperial ambitions. But in course of time the British were compelled in South Arabia to undertake responsibilities, by diplomacy or the judicious use of force, that were far beyond the original intention. They fulfilled their basic purpose in doing so because Aden enjoyed more than a century of peace, only very briefly interrupted during the First World War, and it became prosperous as one of the greatest bunkering ports in the world.

I

Lahej continued to be troublesome for some time. Muhasin's son, Ahmed, pursued a peaceful policy during the two years of his rule from 1847 to 1849, but his son Ali recommenced hostilities which continued intermittently until his tribal force was severely defeated at Sheikh Othman in 1857, whereupon the British occupied the sultanate. It was a matter of concern to the British government that the Turks were actively trying to subdue the Yemen and lay claim to the whole of South Arabia; but this had its compensations in that the tribes surrounding Aden, whose peaceful co-operation the British needed, were anxious to prevent their subjection either to the Turks or to the unorthodox Zeidi Imams of Yemen. Nine tribes therefore accepted British protection, although without formal treaty. The Ottoman government accepted the arrangement *de facto*, the nine tribal areas becoming known in diplomatic parlance as the Nine Cantons. In 1886, the British government signed a formal treaty of protection with the Mahra Sultan of Qishn-Socotra; and, in 1887, Sultan Fadhl ibn Ali of Lahej agreed to accept British protection in return for a monthly stipend of 1,250 Maria Theresa dollars.

This long-lived Sultan of Lahej remained Britain's friend until he met an unfortunate death during the First World War. The Turkish forces advanced on Aden from Taiz, in Yemen, and Fadl loyally assembled his tribesmen to resist them. The British commander in Aden, having in the meanwhile mobilised his troops in Sheikh Othman, marched them seventeen miles across the desert to Lahej, which they reached after several misfortunes, and camped in pouring rain for the night. Next morning they advanced to join the tribesmen who were fighting the Turks. When the Sultan rode towards them alone, they mistook him for a Turk and shot him dead.

The British were forced to withdraw from Lahej and yield part of the Aden Settlement, but the Turkish success was short-lived, enduring only until 1918 when Allied victory on the main fronts forced the Turks to accept the Treaty of Mudros, by the terms of which they withdrew entirely from Arabia. In that year Sultan Abdel Kerim, son of Fadhl, renewed relations with Britain, and Lahej returned to its primary place in what was by that time known as the Western Aden Protectorate. The interlude had its effect on British thinking, however, for there was no question that British protection had failed the Arabs at a crucial moment. It was vital to Britain's standing among the tribes that this should not be allowed to happen again.

During the long peace he maintained in Lahej, the principal state in the Aden hinterland, Sultan Fadhl ibn Ali gave time for the British to create the protectorate system which was to last until they agreed to organise themselves out of it forty years later. There were thirty-one major treaties of protection, the last of which was signed with the Sheikh of the Busi section of the Upper Yafai tribe as late as 1954, by which time there were no less than ninety conventions of various kinds governing British relations with the amirates, sultanates and sheikhdoms of this area, which is only about the size of Great Britain.

After the 1802 treaty with Lahej and the occupation of Aden, the complicated pattern of British relationships was built up piecemeal over a century, but its core was the simple system of protection based on the several treaties, which were almost identical and commendably simple in form. They said, in effect, that Britain granted to the ruler of each territory, and his heirs forever, the gracious favour of protection, in return for which the ruler undertook not to enter into any dealings with other foreign powers, not to sell or cede any of his territory to any power other than Britain, and to notify the British Resident in Aden if any power tried to interfere in the ruler's territories. The states and sheikhdoms brought together by the gracious favour comprised one protectorate, but for convenience they were divided into two regions: the Western and Eastern Protectorate areas.*

These arrangements effectively put all south-western Arabia except Yemen under British guardianship, although only a small territory, the Aden Settlement, was actually possessed by Britain. Even that possession was for so long remotely controlled from Bombay that the Indian lobby in Aden, a powerful merchant and lawyer class, began to dream of its eventual annexation by an independent Indian government. After its conquest in 1839, Aden was attached to the Bombay Presidency; and almost a century later, when provincial autonomy was granted in India, the Arabs feared

---

*The treaties of protection ultimately covered the following. *Western Aden Protectorate*: The sultanate of Lahej, the Alawi sheikhdom, the amirate of Dhala, the Aqrabi sheikhdom, the Audhali sultanate, the Upper and Lower Aulaqi sultanates and the Upper Aulaqi sheikhdom, the amirate of Beihan, the Fadhli sultanate, the Haushabi sultanate, the Dathina confederation, the Upper and Lower Yafai sultanates, the Shaib sheikhdom, the Qutaibi dependency of Dhala, and five petty sheikhdoms of the Upper Yafai region—the Busi, Maflahi, Hadrami, Dhubi and Mausatta. *Eastern Aden Protectorate*: the sultanate of Shihr and Mukalla, the Kathiri sultanate, the Mahra sultanate of Qishn and Socotra, the Wahidi sultanate of Balhaf and Azzan, and the Wahidi sultanate of Bir Ali.

that Bombay would take over Aden and that British officials would be replaced by Indians who, as a community, were neither admired nor liked. This danger was averted in 1932 by making it a 'Chief Commissioner's Province' under the central government of India. Even this did not satisfy the Adenis, who asked that the Settlement should come under the Colonial Office, which had been responsible for relations with the Protectorate areas since 1928, and the Adeni leaders opened successful negotiations with the British by which the Settlement became the Colony of Aden in 1937. A generation ago this development was regarded as an act of liberation.

The British government took possession or control of the main islands off southern Arabia during the century in which it created the protectorate system. Perim, which guards the entrance to the Red Sea and lies 100 miles off Aden, was occupied in 1857 and became part of the Settlement and then the Colony. Socotra, the largest island in the archipelago and lying about 220 miles from the Arabian coast (but only 120 miles off the African coast, nearly opposite the Eastern Horn which ends in Cape Gardafui), was part of the domains of the Mahra Sultan who in 1876 undertook not to alienate any of his possessions except to the British, and then ten years later signed a treaty of protection. This brought Socotra into the Eastern Protectorate. The five Kuria Muria Islands lying off the coast of Muscat were ceded to the British by its Sultan in 1854, becoming technically part of the Aden Settlement; but they were so far away from Aden that they were administered by the British Resident in the Persian Gulf. The Lighthouse Islands were taken by the British in 1915, when they ousted the Turks and installed Arab staffs to maintain the lighthouses. These had been erected and maintained by the French, who had obtained the concession to do so from the Ottoman Sultan in 1899.

Kamaran Island, one of a group which lies off the Salif peninsula of Yemen about 200 miles north of Perim and the Straits of Mandeb, was occupied by the Portuguese in the sixteenth century, but in the nineteenth century it was taken by the Turks, who built a quarantine station on it for pilgrims coming from Africa to Mecca. The British captured the island with troops from Aden in 1915, but did nothing to formalise ownership or protection. The Treaty of Lausanne ended Turkish sovereignty over the group of islands, and Article 16 declared that their 'future . . . will be settled by the parties concerned'; but, as the parties concerned were never specified, no agreement over Kamaran could be reached. The British settled the matter to their own satisfaction in 1949 by an Order in Council which made the Governor of Aden the Governor of Kamaran, with authority to appoint a Commissioner for the group of islands. Kamaran did not become part of the Aden Colony, but for convenience the governor used armed police from Aden for its protection. The Imam of Yemen never recognised this arrangement.

II

The election of Yahya as the Imam of Yemen in 1903 opened the penultimate chapter of Turkish history in South Arabia and prefaced new troubles for Britain. Almost immediately he launched his entire people in a revolt against the Turks which lasted into the next year, and when he was defeated he took time off to prepare another uprising, which broke out in 1911. Although the Turks were again victorious in the merciless guerrilla fighting in the highlands, they had had enough. They established the old division between the Shafei Muslims of the coastal plain and the Zeidi hill region, giving Imam Yahya independence in the latter with the right to appoint provincial governors, and retaining Turkish authority in the plain. This uneasy balance lasted until 1918, when the Ottoman empire collapsed and Yemen at last regained its independence.

Unlike the Arabs to the north who united under the Hashemite rulers of Mecca to ride with Lawrence in revolt against the Turks, the Imam Yahya remained loyal to his erstwhile enemies. The British therefore helped the Idrisi Arabs to occupy the adjoining territory of Asir, and in 1918 took the Yemeni port of Hodeida themselves. When they withdrew in 1921 they handed Hodeida to the Idrisi.

There would certainly have been conflict between the ambitions of Imam Yahya and the geographical requirements of the British in South Arabia, but these incidents exacerbated a natural enmity. He regarded Asir as part of his territory, and when Abdel Aziz ibn Saud overthrew the Hashemites and extended his rule into the Hedjaz, Yahya tried unsuccessfully to prevent him from taking Asir. He was, able, however, to drive the hard-pressed Idrisi from Hodeida and the coastal plain in 1925, thereby uniting the two parts of Yemen once again.

For years before the First World War, the British government had sought to demarcate the frontiers of the Protectorate area southeast of Yemen by agreement with the Turks, and in 1914 they finally signed a convention with the Porte.* Yahya refused to accept either the convention or the British occupation of Kamaran Island. In 1919, the British sent the Assistant Resident of Aden, Lieutenant-Colonel Jacob, on a mission to Sanaa from Hodeida for the purpose of negotiating with the Imam, but he never reached his destination. He was seized at Bajil by the Quhra tribe of Shafei Muslims who feared that the mission would help the Zeidi Imam to reoccupy the Tihamah, and he was detained for four months before being allowed to return to Aden.

Imam Yahya began to intervene in the Protectorates in the following year and quickly over-ran Dhala. The British were slow to fulfil their responsibilities under the protecting treaties; in 1923, the Yemenis took Baidha and, in the following year, the Upper Audhali area. In 1926, they occupied part of Lower Audhali territory, but by this time the British were more prepared and drove them out by air action. By using aircraft again in 1928, the British forced the Yemenis to withdraw from most of the Dhala Amirate.

Sir Gilbert Clayton had attempted to negotiate an agreement about the frontiers in Sanaa in 1926, but the Imam, who not only had considerable territorial gains to encourage him but had also signed a treaty with Italy by which he considered he had strengthened himself against Britain, claimed a large part of the Protectorate area together with Aden, contending that the region was his by right, in the first place, because Yemen had possessed it for a hundred years in the seventeenth and eighteenth centuries; and

*This agreement established the 'Violet Line' marking the Protectorate-Yemen frontier. The Aden government thereafter based itself on this line.

secondly, because he was in any case the rightful heir to the territories in South Arabia relinquished by the Ottoman empire.

In 1928, Yahya signed another treaty, this time with the USSR, but by now the tide was running against him. The forces of King Abdel Aziz ibn Saud were a growing threat and the manifestation of British air strength had reinforced the tribes against him. This made him more amenable to discussion when Sir Bernard Reilly, the British Resident in Aden, reopened negotiations in 1933. In the following year King Abdel Aziz's bedouin force routed Imam Yahya's army, forcing him to sign the Treaty of Taif. Saudi Arabia annexed Asir.

In these adverse circumstances there was little the Imam could do but come to terms with Sir Bernard. In the agreement they signed on February 11, 1934, neither side renounced any of its claims but accepted a *de facto* stabilisation of the frontiers on the basis of the 1914 Anglo-Turkish convention.* Yemen evacuated sixty-four Audhali and eight Dhala villages, released prisoners and hostages taken from the Protectorate, and agreed to reopen the trade route between Yemen and Aden. This completed the liberation of the Audhali and Dhala territories; but the Yemenis continued to hold Baidha, which, though on the Protectorate side of the 1914 frontier, has no protecting treaty with Britain.

The Imam and the Resident in Aden appointed frontier officers to deal with incidents on the spot, and for some years the borders were free of serious trouble. The Imam appointed an agent to Aden but would only allow 'a political clerk' from the Aden administration to be established in Hodeida, and when any important problem arose a high official had to be sent to Sanaa. He did not appoint a representative to London, which was provided for in the agreement, but in 1937 he sent one of his sons to attend the coronation of King George VI and allowed the Church of Scotland's 'Keith Falconer Medical Mission' to send one of its teams to Sanaa, where

*The agreement for the first time called the Imam the King of Yemen and recognised his independence. He was afterwards still generally referred to as the Imam, and I have kept to that designation as it reflected also his religious authority.

it remained until 1943. It was, nevertheless, always an uneasy relationship and could not by any means be called friendly.

III

During this period of truce with Yemen, the Aden government gave its mind to the pacification of the Protectorate areas, where conditions in the hill country came close to anarchy. Personal vendettas and family blood feuds were rife, and the rulers, frequently challenged by brothers and cousins, exercised only a minimal control of their peoples. Aden had become an Air Command in 1928 and, to replace British infantry for ground operations, tribesmen were organised and trained in several formations, known as Tribal Guards. These were recruited in each tribal area and operated under the command of their own chieftains. A civil internal security force, known as the Government Guards, was formed under British and Arab officers and financed by the British government. Then, in 1934, a military force, the Aden Protectorate Levies, was recruited from the tribesmen of the Western Protectorate, officered again by British and Arabs and controlled by the British military commander in Aden. For several years thereafter, the Levies were able to control the region without any support from British troops.

The role of the Royal Air Force based on Aden was to fly to the support of Tribal Guards or Levies whenever they needed help, but perhaps an even more important function was to provide fast communications between Aden and the various parts of the Protectorate, for up to that time news of a tribal war or a heavy frontier raid could take days over mountain and desert tracks and dirt roads before it reached the seat of government. The RAF was able to impose its rough and ready peace very rapidly, as the Imam of Yemen discovered almost at once.

Up to this time, the British were concerned almost exclusively with the Western Protectorate area. Although in theory there was only one Protectorate,* the wealthier, larger and more populous

---

*The description of 'Eastern' and 'Western' Protectorates had almost become formal by the fact that each region had its Political Adviser and a degree of separate administration in Aden.

Eastern area was of less concern because it was further away from Aden. As long as the tribal states there were not threatened from outside and did not enter into any dealings forbidden to them by the protecting treaties, the British Colonial Office was prepared to let the innumerable tribes enjoy their feuds, fights and general anarchy, for there had not been peace among the tribes or on the roads for centuries. The visits of Residents from Aden to the rulers were perfunctory affairs, described by Harold Ingrams as of the 'How d'you do–Goodbye' variety,* and the great Hadramaut valley was unknown to all but a few intrepid explorers. There was no question of oil or other natural wealth. Nothing was further from the mind of Whitehall than an 'imperial mission', for the area seemed likely to cost time, trouble and money to no particular purpose. A frontier claim of Saudi Arabia was the only external reason for intervention. Had the British Resident in Aden not decided that it was time he knew more about this large area which Britain was committed to protect, and had he not chosen to send there a man—Harold Ingrams—who had developed a passionate interest in the Hadramaut from Hadraumis he had met while serving the Colonial Office in Zanzibar, the area might have continued to waste away in its brooding hates for many more years to come.

This Eastern Protectorate region covered about 68,000 square miles, and in the 1930s it probably had a population of about 200,000 people. Its coastline stretched for about 400 miles from the Lower Aulaqi sultanate to the western border of Muscat and Oman, and it was about 250 miles wide at its broadest point where it reached the sands of the great desert, the Rub al-Khali—the Empty Quarter. The most important state was the Qaiti sultanate of Shihr and Mukalla, whose ruler had been dignified by the British with the title of His Highness and the right to an eleven-gun salute. It had by far the highest income of any state either in the Eastern or Western

*Harold Ingrams, *Arabia and the Isles*, 1966. Anyone writing about the Hadramaut in the key period of the 1930s must refer to this book, because only Ingrams and his wife could tell the story in detail. I shall therefore not acknowledge it again in this chapter and direct quotations are from this book unless otherwise noted.

regions. The Wahidi sultanate of Balhaf and Azzan, with the tiny Wahidi sultanate of Bir Ali, was sandwiched between the Qaiti and the Lower Aulaqi states, and the Mahra sultanate of Qishn and Socotra lay between the Qaiti eastern border and the sultanate of Muscat and Oman. Inland from the Qaiti state was the Kathiri sultanate, which shared with it the Wadi Hadramaut and was the second most important state in the region.

Wadi Hadramaut is the most distinctive feature of south-west Arabia. Its wide upper and middle reaches run almost parallel with the coast at about 125 miles distance inland, but at the lower end it turns sharply to the south-east and becomes a narrow cut through the hills as it descends to the coastal plain and the sea at Sayhut, in the Qaiti sultanate. The wide inland section can get up to 30 inches of rain in the summer, and seasonal torrents have cut deep ravines—often contained between imposing cliffs on each side of the wadi—just as the outflow has cut the lower narrow valley to the sea.

The Hadramaut is the best expanse of agricultural land in South Arabia. It is surrounded by barren deserts and hills in the Wahidi sultanate, the northern Kathiri desert, the barren hills and plains of the Mahra sultanate and the central mountains of the Qaiti state—all of which shelter it from the outside world. At various periods of the ancient kingdoms it had been extremely prosperous, and throughout history it has been, like some parts of the coastal plain, a settled land of expert farmers; but they were an adventurous and talented people who travelled and settled far and wide, in the Hedjaz, in Egypt, in the Sudan, Zanzibar and Ethiopia, and later, when the steamship came, in Indonesia and Singapore where they became an extremely rich community. Remittances from the emigrant families are still an important, if declining, source of wealth to the Qaiti and Kathiri states.

Until quite recently, the Sultan of Shihr and Mukalla, so called because these were his two major towns on the coast, spent most of his time in India and his authority scarcely touched the Wadi Hadramaut, where even the smallest village was built defensively against the many enemies without. The houses rose six or eight storeys into the air with the ground floor used to shelter the animals, but also protecting the upper storeys by a maze of winding narrow passages which gave access to the stairs. Having lived for centuries without law, the whole region was torn with feuds between tribes and subtribes, between villages, and even between families, and fighting had ruined the agriculture of the valley. Ingrams describes many examples: of a man who could speak only from his second-floor window because he was conducting a private war against his neighbours; of villagers who had to cut a trench to fields out of rifle range so they could travel to them under cover; of people who had not left their house for eighteen or twenty-one years. Almost everywhere trenches were dug for the purpose of war. The primitive roads and tracks were beset by marauding tribesmen who were often nomads from the distant sands. As background to this anarchy there was the bitter enmity between the ruling families of the Qaiti and Kathiri sultanates.

Ingrams first went there in 1934, returning in 1936 with the blessing of the British Resident in Aden and a limited purpose: 'To help the people to get out of the mess they were in.' This enterprise was all the more remarkable because the Aden government had not given him the slightest reason to think he would get any forces to impose his will, while the Qaiti Sultan had only 200 unruly Yafai mercenaries as a regular army and no intention to try to extend his authority from the coastal plain. The people had contempt for all sultans and hatred of their spasmodic tyrannies.

Nevertheless, Ingrams set about persuading them to sign a truce that would cover all past offences and preserve future peace. He found that they were all sick to death of the interminable feuding. Their simple request, which he was quite unable to answer, was for Britain to put in troops or send planes to enforce any truce they signed on both sultans and tribes alike. Otherwise they could not see any peace agreement being worth the paper it was written on. There was no passionate national objection to British intervention, such as was soon to bedevil British efforts everywhere. On the contrary, the people were in general willing to see the most troublesome marauding tribes bombed into submission; and, at the higher level, the Qaiti Sultan was quite willing to become part of the British empire.

When Ingrams, advancing from Mukalla on his mission, looked down from the cliff top on the white palaces and minarets of Tarim, the chief city of the Hadramaut, there was not much practical support for him beyond the friendship and devotion to peace of Sayyid Bubakr bin Sheikh al-Kaf of Tarim, who had retired from South-East Asia to his beloved valley with a considerable fortune, which he was willing to spend for the betterment of the people. With his support, Ingrams and his wife toured the nearby towns, including the important centre of Shibam, spreading their gospel of peace. His success against all the odds was so great that his first report frightened the Aden authorities, and they warned him that he must not enter into any commitments.

By then it was already too late. Those tribal leaders gathered together by Ingrams at Seiyun, between Tarim and Shibam, had reached the stage of discussing a truce and were disputing how long it should last in the first instance. They wanted only six months to see if Britain would intervene to make it work, but Ingrams stood out for three years and eventually got them. The first peace meeting was concluded on February 6, 1937, by which time the Aden government had given some proof of its support by bombing a village of the Ban Yamani tribe who had made the mistake of attacking the convoy of an engineer officer sent to survey a road for the Sultan. The bombing greatly pleased the tribes and villages because the Ban Yamani had been constantly troublesome on the roads. Immediately after the peace meeting, the leaders of the tribe came in with their fines and hostages and made peace. To Ingrams they said: 'You did well to bomb us. And we thank you. If we had given in before, the people would have said we were cowards. We want peace, too, now that we know you'll keep it.'

In the ensuing weeks the truce spread far and wide through the tribes and towns until, by the time the rains came in April, about 1,400 signatures committed the people to keep peace among themselves and the roads free to travellers. The rains were heavy that year and this was taken as a good omen and God's reward for the truce, which has ever since been known among Arab and foreigners alike as 'Ingrams' Peace'. From that date in 1937 it became possible to help the states to organise and administer their territories.

There were obviously many years of hard work ahead. Not only had courts of justice and government departments to be established, but first the people had to be found and trained to run them. In the midst of this, Mr and Mrs Ingrams tackled the question of the slaves owned mainly by the Qaiti and Kathiri Sultans and were successful in having slavery made illegal. In the case of the Sultans, the slaves had become such a privileged group that their liberation removed a social nuisance; but among the tribes there was still cruelty and oppression. In April 1938, the commander of the Aden Protectorate Levies was sent to advise on the small Mukalla regular army, and he later seconded an officer to train it. In July, the first motor road was opened linking Shihr and Mukalla on the coast with Tarim, Shibam and Seiyun in the Hadramaut: a blessing to the cultivators of the great valley, supplementing the safety of travel brought to them by the truce.

Early in August 1938, the Qaiti Sultan signed a new treaty with the British government under which he accepted a Resident Adviser. This was the first of the advisory treaties which became the system by which the Aden government was able to establish its influence in the Protectorate area as a whole. It also confirmed the succession of the Sultan's family. Harold Ingrams became Resident Adviser in the Qaiti and Kathiri Sultans, and he was given charge of the entire Eastern Protectorate area.

From the beginning, the arrangements for protection had all the peculiarities of a British compromise which had developed in make-shift fashion over the years. No attempt was made to take possession of the protectorate states, but in practice the Aden government imposed its will whenever it felt that security was threatened or one of the friendly tribal rulers was in danger. By acting in this way the Aden authorities 'froze' the tribal leaderships in the hands of those who happened to be in power at the time, but only for as long as they remained faithful to their treaty commitments. As the experienced officials in Aden knew, this practical arrangement was not true to the system of the tribes, who liked to get rid of a ruler who proved weak or vicious in favour of his brother or cousin whom they thought more fit to lead: a primitive democratic choice which was no longer possible if the British stepped in to prevent it.

How the system worked is described by Sir Tom Hickinbotham, a former Governor of Aden, in the case of a man called Alawi Ahmed of Beihan:

> ... he was in disgrace for an outrage against the Sharif of Beihan and had had to be taken very severely to task. He had been called upon to come to Aden and answer for his sins to the Political Secretary, and when he had failed to appear had been ordered to pay a quite substantial fine by a given date, and as he had failed to pay the fine air action had been taken against his property, that is to say, against his fortified house and damage to the extent of the fine had been done. It was an established procedure in such cases, and honour was satisfied, and normally there were no complaints. . . .*

As the nature of the outrage is not stated, this may well have been a justified punishment, but the 'established procedure' was used against anyone, perhaps a member of the family with a better claim to rule, who opposed the chief whom the British protected, and this was to have its disadvantages in time when discontented members of ruling families went over the frontier to Yemen to join the Imam against their ruling relatives.

The Sharif of Beihan was one of the rulers whose position was considered by many to be entirely a creation of the British. It was claimed that, since the British could not get the Masabein and Bel Harith (two of the great tribes of Beihan) to sign a protectorate treaty, they persuaded the Habili leader, Ahmed am-Mohsin, to sign a document in 1903 putting the territories of the two tribes under protection. He was then given military support to consolidate his power in the whole of Beihan, and the paramount sheikhs of the Masabein and Bel Harith subsequently spent a great part of their time being 'dissidents' in Yemen or Saudi Arabia. There were other leaders in Yemen, such as Amir Haidara of Dhala, who were dissident because they were deposed by the British, but were still

*Sir Tom Hickinbotham, *Aden*, 1958, p. 53.

27

thought by many tribesmen to be the true rulers. Amir Haidara, for example, was considered to have more right to rule Dhala than Amir Shaaful who replaced him.

The system of collective punishment was used with considerable effect against marauding subtribes who plundered caravans or committed other tribal crimes, but in every case the offenders were given notice to evacuate themselves, their women, their children, their animals and as much movable property as they could before the punitive air strike took place, so that there were seldom casualties as there certainly would have been if an attempt had been made to punish a village by ground troops. The method had the support of the Aden authorities, and in time it greatly reduced the number of outrages and the general disorder of the territory.

Another Aden Governor, Sir Bernard Reilly, commented:

It is a form of collective punishment, but that is understood and not resented by tribesmen who, in a country without regular police, would refuse to surrender an individual culprit.

Pacification of a country unaccustomed to orderly government could not be effected without collective punishment of collective acts of violence such as brigandage, but as the work of pacification proceeded the need for the intervention of the Royal Air Force became rarer. The institution of Government and Tribal Guards proved a success. It strengthened the hands of the Government and the hands of the local rulers, and the enlistment of Protectorate tribesmen in these units and the Aden Protectorate Levies gave these men a new conception of disciplined loyalty and of the value of the preservation of peace.*

It was inevitable that, in offering this security to the rulers, the British should more and more come to require them to behave in a reasonable way, for 'the established procedure' of pacification was not intended to be *carte blanche* for any form of misgovernment. The problem was to decide where primitive tribal custom ended and

---

*Sir Bernard Reilly, *Aden and the Yemen*, 1960, p. 21. Sir Bernard's period of service occurred before the transistor radio and the insurgent nationalism of Arab radio broadcasts had begun to erode even disciplined loyalties.

misgovernment began, and the British government was still determined not to make itself responsible for administering innumerable
tribes and subtribes. Over the years, the answer to the problem
began to emerge of its own accord in that rulers desiring to maintain
British protection for themselves and their people became amenable
to British advice, at least on major issues. Some time after the Treaty
of Sanaa in 1934, the Aden government began to regularise the
position by making advisory treaties to supplement the protecting
treaties in the main states of the region, on the pattern of that
agreed by Harold Ingrams in the Eastern Protectorate with the
Qaiti and Kathiri Sultans. The Second World War interrupted the
process but, by 1954, thirteen advisory treaties had been signed.*

The advisory, like the protecting, treaties were simple in form,
binding the rulers to accept the advice of the Governor of Aden. In
those signed by the Qaiti Sultan of Shihr and Mukalla, the Kathiri
Sultan of Seiyun, and the Mahra Sultan of Qishn and Socotra,
tribal custom and the Muslim religion were subjects excluded from
the rulers' commitments, but these states accepted a resident
British Political Adviser, as did the Sultan of Lahej. Neither the
Colonial Office nor the Aden government ever contemplated direct
administration of the protectorate areas, even where Resident
Advisers were appointed. These officers were given the most limited
powers and were directed at all times to strengthen the authority of
the rulers and assist them to introduce workable administrations for
the simple public services the states possessed, so that through them
development aid could be channelled.

The treaties had the disadvantage that Britain and the Aden
government were blamed for the shortcomings of the states, for
their backwardness and for the failure of the rulers to permit
progress fast enough. Arabs in more advanced countries either

*The list of advisory treaties is as follows. *Western Protectorate*: in 1944 and
1945, the Sultans of Fadhli, Lower Aulaqi, Haushabi and Lower Yafai, the
Sharif of Beihan and the Amir of Dhala; in 1951, the Sheikh of Upper Aulaqi, the
Sultan of Audhali and the Sultan of Lahej. *Eastern Protectorate*: in 1938, the
Sultans of Qaiti and Kathiri; in 1949, the Wahidi Sultan of Balhaf in 1949;
and in 1954, the Sultan of Qishn and Socotra.

refused to see or did not see much difference between a protected state and a colony. In the sense that the rulers' powers were circumscribed, the difference was not great and where it did exist was adverse because the Aden government had neither the men nor the administrative machinery to impose its will even on all matters coming within the field of its right to advise.

In time, criticism of Britain's failure to increase the speed of progress and limit the arbitrariness of certain of the rulers' behaviour spread to some of the people of the protected states themselves. Ironically, it was Aden that encouraged this discontent, for it was from its free port that cheap transistor radios flooded the tribal areas, where willing ears listened to the political broadcasts of Egypt and other Arab countries.

The advisory treaties superimposed on protection completed the arrangements made by Britain in the Eastern and Western Protectorates. The Governor of Aden fulfilled his responsibilities for protection and advice with the help of two Political Agents, one for each Protectorate area, and of the advisers attached to the agents and to some of the rulers. Even before the last advisory agreement was signed in 1954, expert opinion in the British administration recognised the deficiencies of the system and was beginning to think of federation.

IV

In Aden itself there was a parallel trend of thought in the direction of giving the people a greater part in government. When the Settlement became a Colony in 1937, it was given the normal form of colonial administration, with a Governor, who was also commander-in-chief of the forces, aided by an Executive Council. By the Aden Colony (Amendment) Order of 1947, a Legislative Council was constituted, but without any elected members. The Governor alone decided what matters should be brought before the Executive Council and he was not compelled to submit matters he preferred to reserve for himself, but if he did refer to the Legislative Council he was required to take the majority opinion or, if he rejected it, to submit the reasons for his rejection to the Secretary of State for the Colonies.

For nearly twenty years, there was never any need to oppose the decisions of the Legislative Council, the membership of which was half official (the Chief Secretary, the Attorney General, the Financial Secretary, the Assistant Chief Secretary for the Colony, and a representative of the commander of the British armed forces), and the remainder worthy, elderly gentlemen chosen as representatives of their particular communities. These men could hardly be considered an opposition to official opinion; on the contrary, they were proud to consider themselves part of the Aden government and for many years never gave a thought to the idea of elections or self-government. It was not until 1950 that Sir Tom Hickinbotham, then chairman of the Port Trust and leader of the group of unofficial members, referred to the feeling that perhaps some changes should be made to allow articulate and critical younger members of the communities some say in their affairs. Addressing the Legislative Council, he said: 'At the same time I feel it my duty to say that we realise that in the not too distant future an awakening sense of responsibility among the younger members of the community may justify Your Excellency's successor in making changes in the membership on the unofficial side of the council. If and when that time comes . . . we will be very willing and ready to do all that we can to co-operate.'* This modest hint of things to come bore fruit five years later when the constitution was again amended to permit the election of a minority of the Legislative Council members.

The amendment was already too little and too late, and bore witness to the failure of the government to understand the ferment in the minds of many people in the Colony. The only opinion taken seriously was that of the influential merchant class, which was prospering exceedingly under British rule and therefore saw no reason for change except in the direction of securing more power for itself within the Colony, or at least in association with Britain.

There was not much organised political opinion up to the

*Hickinbotham, op. cit. He was himself the successor called on to make the change.

31

mid-1950s, though one can distinguish three political groups. The oldest of these was the *Aden Association*, which largely represented merchant opinion, stood for Aden for the Adenese, and was willing to co-operate with Britain for peaceful constitutional advance; some of the members of the association at the time wanted Aden to remain within the British Commonwealth. It was significant that they were willing to consider as Adenese all Indians, Pakistanis and Somalis who had made their homes in the Colony for a generation, for these constituted substantial Commonwealth minorities in the trading and professional community to whom, later, the majority of Adenese desired to deny the franchise. The *United National Front* was a vociferous minority party demanding the total elimination of British rule and the merger of Aden, the Protectorates and Yemen, and even Muscat and Oman, into a single independent state. Although it was a minority group, it had connections with the burgeoning trade-union movement which gave it some power to disturb the peace by strikes, and it was regarded by the government and the Aden Association as an irresponsible rabble. The *South Arabian League* had its genesis in Lahej and reflected the desire of the Sultan of Lahej to establish his pre-eminence in the region, for it advocated the merger of Aden and the Protectorates, but not Yemen, in to a single state independent of Britain. (For further discussion of Adeni political groups, see chapter 4.)

None of these embryo organisations could command majority support, and the weekly press—which largely reflected merchant views—for long concentrated only on the demand for municipal elections, justifying their conservatism on the grounds that the people were not ready for democracy and required some training in a limited field of public affairs. This was not the view of the educated and half-educated younger element in Aden, many of whom came from merchant families. If they did not want either the United National Front or the South Arabian League to gain ground, they certainly desired faster progress towards self-government in the Colony than the Aden Association advocated. It would not have been easy, and perhaps was impossible, for the Aden government to nurture 'moderate progressive' opinion, but the failure to establish a balance between it and the Aden Association eventually drove some of the younger people into more extreme movements and destroyed the influence of the others.

When the elections for the few seats in the Legislative Council took place in December 1955, the Aden Association won and the South Arabian League's candidates failed outright. The United National Front campaigned for a boycott of the elections but this also failed and the polling took place in orderly fashion. (The Front subsequently concentrated on strengthening its hold on the labour and trade-union movements.)

By this time, however, there was a powerful external influence in the Colony. The course of the Egyptian revolution, which had taken place in July 1952, had been followed with close interest by Adeni Arabs and by 1955 President Nasser's star was well in the ascendant. His success in securing the agreement for British evacuation of the Canal Zone in 1954 and his arms deal with the Russians in 1955 were taken as signs by many people in Aden that a new and great leader had arisen in the Arab world; even conservatives in the Aden Association could not but admire his single-handed struggle for total emancipation. As a result, the message of insurgent nationalism from Radio Cairo was widely listened to in the Colony and was soon so feared by the government that plans to counter it from an Aden Broadcasting Station were rapidly, but ineffectively, prepared.*

The response of the Colonial Office and the Aden government was to make sure that no one in the Colony should take the limited popular representation in the Legislative Council to mean that Aden was set on a rapid course towards democracy. Lord Lloyd, the Minister of State at the Colonial Office, visited Aden in May 1956, and was greeted by a demonstration at the airport calling for

*Cf. Gillian King, *Imperial Outpost—Aden*, Chatham House Essay, Oxford University Press, 1964, p. 59. 'The range of Aden Broadcasting Station was only increased from 50 to some 1,000 miles in 1958: the Government's reason for the delay being that the cost of the new equipment would be some £20,000 more than it was prepared to pay. Even by 1962 broadcasting from Aden was limited in output and of low quality, because the budget allocation was not sufficient to buy better programmes. Radio Cairo and Sanaa meanwhile broadcast almost continuously.'

independence—the first time a distinguished visitor had been so received. He made the following public statement while in Aden:

There has been much speculation recently about the political future of the Colony of Aden. Such speculation, if unrelated to practical possibilities, is harmful to the commercial interests of the Colony upon which the prosperity and, indeed, the whole livelihood of the people depends: if carried to undue lengths it can easily divert into unfruitful channels energies which might be better exerted in the pursuit of reasonable aspirations. Her Majesty's Government consider, therefore, that the time has come when their political intentions in respect of the Colony should be clearly stated, and my visit to the Colony has seemed to them a suitable opportunity for this purpose. I have had discussions with various representative bodies on matters affecting further constitutional development; I have listened to their views with interest and sympathy. Last January there was a most important political development when elected members of this Council took their seats for the first time. Her Majesty's Government sincerely welcome this advance, but it needs to be fully tested before further advance can be considered. Certainly there could be no question of any further radical change in the constitution during the life of the present Council. The degree of constitutional development and the pace at which it can be realised must depend on the sense of responsibility which is displayed by the people of the Colony and their leaders. There is no reason why you cannot expect to achieve further constitutional development in due course. Many of you have a perfectly legitimate desire to take a greater part in the affairs of Government, and there is no reason why this desire should not be realised. But I should like you to understand that for the foreseeable future it would not be reasonable or sensible, or indeed in the interests of the Colony's inhabitants, for them to aspire to any aim beyond that of a considerable degree of internal self-government. Therefore, whilst I have indicated the type of constitutional advance to which the people in this Colony may legitimately aspire, Her Majesty's

Government wish to make it clear that the importance of Aden both strategically and economically within the Commonwealth is such that they cannot foresee the possibility of any fundamental relaxation of their responsibilities for the Colony. I feel that this assurance will be welcome to you and to the vast majority of the Colony.*

This statement reassured the merchant class but greatly displeased the growing body of radical nationalists. Radio Cairo responded with vitriolic criticism of British colonial policy in South Arabia and called for a revolt of all the people there. As a statement of policy it was already verging on the unreal, for the planning of a federation of South Arabia was underway and was firmly fixed in many minds as the next stage of development. It was hardly possible that a federation could exist without Aden, and it was equally unlikely that Aden could remain a colony or constitutional advance be unduly delayed if it joined.

*Reilly, op. cit., pp. 44–45.

3

The Arab Amirates of the South

IMAM YAHYA behaved with surprising moderation during the Second World War, preserving a strict neutrality and postponing his claim at a time when he might well have embarrassed Britain. He nevertheless protested strongly against a Free Yemeni movement which had established itself in Aden under one of his sons; and the fact that the British 'did not feel able to interfere with or suppress these Yemeni malcontents as long as they confined themselves to expression of opinion'* did not encourage post-war conciliation.

The Imam's concern was justified. The Free Yemeni movement was working in close association with Sayyid Abdullah ibn Ahmed al-Wazir, who headed a rebellion in Sanaa in February 1948 and was proclaimed Imam by an assembly of religious leaders.† A few days later, on February 17, Imam Yahya, then aged eighty, was assassinated and two of his sons were killed defending his treasury.‡ The

*Reilly, op. cit., p. 23.

†Al-Wazir belonged to a branch of the ruling family which had once held the Imamate and had usually had an important position in the state. Yahya had made the mistake of excluding him from high office for, although the Free Yemenis were mostly disgruntled Shafeis, they turned to this leading Zeidi as one likely to command Zeidi support against Yahya.

‡'After the assassination of Imam Yahya so many Shafeis fled to Aden that the Government advised them to move-on. Most of them went to either Pakistan or Egypt', Hickinbotham, op. cit., p. 75. Reilly (op. cit., p. 25) states that the plot was not hatched in Aden, but Mohammed Ali Luqman—a leading journalist and newspaper proprietor in Aden, who sympathised with the Free Yemeni movement and was in close touch with it—cabled the British-owned Arab News Agency an assassination account almost exactly as it happened *a week before it happened.*

36

rebellion was short-lived. Amir Seif al-Islam Ahmed, Yahya's son and heir-apparent, who was Governor of Taiz, mobilised a force of loyal tribes, recaptured Sanaa and was elected Imam on March 13. He executed al-Wazir and thirty of his adherents. Ahmed was fifty-six years old.

In his last few years, Yahya had started to take Yemen a little further out of its seclusion. He had joined the newly formed Arab League in 1945, and in the following year he signed treaties of friendship and commerce with the United States, France and Iraq, and allowed two American trade delegations to visit Sanaa. Imam Ahmed was well aware that his father's autocratic and often brutal methods were responsible for the Free Yemeni movement and after the assassination he set out to be more liberal, in so far as that word could be applied to the standards of the country. A writer in *The Economist* described Yemen as 'rushing madly from the thirteenth into the fourteenth century'. He established an advisory council of religious leaders, notables and tribal chiefs and appointed a cabinet of fifteen ministers, although these were mostly sons and close relatives. He sought technical assistance from the United Nations and by 1955 there were fifteen experts studying the country's needs and resources. He also invited the help of other foreign experts and investors; a West German firm was entrusted with exploiting salt mines, an East German firm with the erection of a cement factory, a tannery and textile mills, and the Yemen Development Corporation of America with oil exploration.

I

The reign of Imam Ahmed opened with extreme bitterness towards Britain because of the assassination of his father, which he laid at the door of Aden for tolerating the plotters. He received an official from Aden and spoke of better relations with Britain, but made no secret of his feelings on the matter. He kept the frontier quiet and reappointed frontier officers to prevent trouble, but in doing so his policy was designed to encourage Britain to terminate the Sanaa Treaty of 1934, which still had nearly thirty years to run, and to

C

establish his rule over the whole of South Arabia. His main contention for the moment was that Britain had no right under the treaty to change the internal administration of the Protectorate states from the position that existed in 1934.

Only a few months after he came to power, Ahmed invited Sir Reginald Champion, then Governor of Aden, to visit Taiz where he had established his capital. On Sir Reginald's proposing that Britain and Yemen should exchange diplomatic representatives, Ahmed agreed, but suggested that the Aden Governor should be the British representative. The Foreign Office accepted this unusual arrangement. (The Imam never executed his part of it.) He also asked for an extradition treaty, which was no doubt intended to prevent Aden from becoming a refuge for his opponents, but the impossibility of accepting at face value any judicial verdicts in Yemen compelled Britain to reject the request. The British government was more sympathetic to other requests—for electrical installations, dredgers, a ship, doctors and a road engineer—but not to his application for armoured vehicles, which it believed were intended for use against the Protectorate rulers. Prince Seif al-Islam Abdullah visited London on his way back from the United Nations in pursuit of assistance, but as the conversations proceeded and it became apparent that Imam Ahmed had no intention of conceding any of his claims in South Arabia, there was no practical outcome. In March 1949, trouble occurred on the frontiers again.

The Sharif of Beihan proposed to build a customs post at Nagd Marqad, which is a pass lying between Wadi Harib in Yemen and the northern end of Wadi Beihan, and the Aden government agreed that the site lay three miles within Beihan. Qadi Mohammed al-Shami, the Yemeni frontier officer, not only contended that it lay within Yemen, but that to build a customs house conflicted with the *status quo* of the 1934 treaty. Yemeni troops then began to build a fort at Jabal Manawa, just west of Wadi Marqad and, according to the Aden government, inside Beihan. Even before the fort was completed, they opened fire on the customs house, and at one time the Sharif's men were under attack continuously for two weeks. There were the usual exchanges, of claims and counterclaims. After

British warnings went unheeded, the RAF demolished the half-completed fort and the Yemenis withdrew with their one wounded soldier. The Yemeni Minister in Cairo protested to the British Ambassador that the attack had been made on Yemeni territory, and Prince Abdullah protested to the British Minister of State who was attending the United Nations in New York, and talked of appealing to that body. The Imam called for support from the Arab League and Radio Cairo broadcast indignantly about British aggression.

The British on September 29, 1949 had proposed that boundary markers should be laid to prevent frontier disputes, but Yemen would have nothing to do with this until its claim for Nagd Marqad was admitted and compensation paid for the fort and the wounded man. The Aden government did nothing to improve matters in November when it permitted Petroleum Concessions Limited, a subsidiary of British Petroleum, to send an exploratory party to Shabwa district, which lay 100 miles to the north-east of Beihan. Petroleum Concessions had held the concession for the whole of the Protectorate since 1938, but this was a particularly inappropriate time to make use of it because Shabwa was another area in dispute between the Aden government and Yemen, and an attempt to settle the dispute in 1940 had failed.

Imam Ahmed was challenging Clause 3 of the Sanaa Treaty of 1934 which preserved the *status quo* on the frontiers as they were at the time of the signing of the agreement. The second paragraph of Clause 3 reads:

Pending the conclusion of the negotiations referred to in the preceding paragraph [which deferred a permanent settlement until further negotiations were completed during the forty years' duration of the treaty] the high contracting parties agree to maintain the situation existing in regard to the frontier on the date of the signature of the treaty, and both high contracting parties undertake that they will prevent, by all means at their disposal, any violation by their forces of the above-mentioned frontier, and any interference by their subjects, or from their side of the frontier, with the affairs of the people inhabiting the other side of the frontier.

39

When the Governor of Aden informed the Imam that the British government was willing to discuss whether Nagd Marqad was in the Protectorate or not, but would not pay compensation until the results of the discussion were known and would certainly not discuss administrative arrangements within the Protectorate, he was touching the main issue, for the Imam contended that the *status quo* in the Sanaa Treaty referred to all the conditions prevailing in 1934. He did not reply to the Governor but sent a message to the Foreign Office that he would agree to a conference in London. The two governments agreed to the conference in July 1950, and the British government and the Governor of Aden immediately issued a joint statement declaring that the purposes of the conference were to determine the best procedure for settling the Nagd Marqad and Shabwa disputes, to determine the *status quo* frontier of 1934, to create the conditions for establishing diplomatic relations, and to improve trade relations.

The conference reached an agreement in mid-October 1950 after six weeks of discussion, but it was little more than a *modus vivendi* and the agreement specifically stated that neither side relinquished its claims. Before the conclusion of the conference it had become apparent that Yemen wanted the settlement provided for in the 1934 treaty on the basis of the Imam's right to rule both the Protectorate and Aden, whereas the British contended that, as the successor state of the Ottoman empire, Yemen was bound by the 1914 Anglo-Turkish 'Violet Line' which was therefore the *de jure* frontier. (See page 19.)

The Shabwa affair had further increased the range of difference by arousing Yemen's interest in the possibility of oil there. Shabwa lay north-east of the territory of the Bel Harith tribe where the 1914 frontier definition had ended, and the British argued that, as neither Yemen nor Britain controlled the area north-east of the Bel Harith, there was no *de facto* frontier and that therefore a conference established to discuss the 1934 *status quo* frontier could not study a non-existent line beyond the Bel Harith. Yemen wanted to study the frontier all the way to Shabwa and so to challenge Britain's claim to control the tribal areas that lay beyond the Bel Harith. Shabwa lay south of, but beyond, the 'Violet Line', but Yemen argued that it had a right to all South Arabia except for the temporary exclusion of territory lying south of the line.

The agreement provided for a joint commission to demarcate the frontier on the ground and settle disputes on the basis of it, and further provided that, if agreement could not be reached, an impartial member would be appointed to assist the commission 'to reach a unanimous recommendation', and that the two governments would pursue a settlement in accordance with Article 33 of the UN Charter if they still disagreed with the commission's findings. It was further agreed that, as soon as the commission started work, the Nagd Marqad Customs House would be evacuated (a provision that greatly annoyed the Sharif of Beihan as the Yemenis had built three customs posts on its side of the frontier), and that Yemen would not rebuild and reoccupy the demolished fort. Finally, the two governments undertook to check hostile propaganda and subversive activities, and to study 'at an appropriate time' specific proposals regarding fugitive offenders—a clause which reflected the failure to agree on extradition.

The boundary commission, which was the principal purpose of the conference, was never set up, but the conference agreed that the two governments would establish diplomatic relations, and this part was executed. Yemen sent a Minister to London and the British a Chargé d'Affaires to Taiz, which was the effective capital of Yemen. This meant that British dealings with Yemen were channelled through the Foreign Office instead of the Aden government, which the Imam greatly distrusted. Although the agreement seemed to achieve very little and did not settle any of the outstanding problems between Yemen and the Aden government, it did purchase nearly three years of peace.

II

Although the essential reason for conflict between the Protectorate and Yemen was the Imam's claim to possess the region and the determined opposition of the Shafei Muslims of the region to this claim, the immediate cause of the deterioration of relations at the end of 1953 was the knowledge in Taiz that plans were afoot for a federation of the Protectorate states.

The originator of the plan was Mr G. K. N. Trevaskis,* Political Agent and Adviser for the Western Protectorate, who drafted the first plan in 1950. He presented it to Sir Tom Hickinbotham, then Governor of Aden, who discussed it with his advisers and, on submitting it in an amended form to the Minister of State at the Colonial Office in London, received authority to submit it to the rulers. It provided for two separate federal areas, one for the Eastern Protectorate and the other for the Western: an arrangement which took account of the more advanced development in the Eastern region, its different historical background, and its tendency not to co-operate with the Western. Each federation would have a Council of Rulers which would meet as and when necessary, and also a Working Committee to which each ruler would nominate three members and which would have power to make decisions on behalf of the Council. Below the Council of Ministers and its Working Committee there would be Executive and Legislative Councils to which members would be nominated until such time as it was thought possible to hold elections. In the case of the Eastern Federation, it was proposed that the Mahra sultanate of Qishn and Socotra and the tiny state of Bir Ali should be excluded at the outset, the former because it was not administratively as well developed as the other major states and the latter because it was too small.

The federal authorities would not be concerned with the internal affairs of each members state, but it was hoped that in time the rulers would see the advantage of central government and transfer more and more of their domestic responsibilities to it. This exclusion left the federal administrations responsible for communications, health and education (all of which were subject already to advice from Aden and lent themselves to central direction), and customs, which were still levied individually by all the states and were intended to be the source of finance for the federations.

*Later Sir Kennedy Trevaskis, High Commissioner of Aden. Amir Ahmed bin Abdullah of the Fadhli sultanate said at the inauguration of the Federation in 1959 that the idea was conceived fifteen years earlier.

The head of both federations was to be the Governor of Aden, with the title of High Commissioner; but, while retaining this over-all responsibility, the British government did not want to increase the modest £800,000 yearly subsidy which was paid to the Protectorates to maintain the Government Guards and Hadhrami Bedouin Legion, the internal security arrangements of the individual states, and in certain cases the state administrations. The centralisation of customs was intended to be an administrative economy by eliminating the twenty-five customs organisations of the individual states, and it was hoped that with these savings, together with the imposition of realistic import and export duties, it would be possible to meet the federal costs and compensate the states for their loss of customs revenue. It was further expected that Aden Colony would help. The Protectorate states suffered from the fact that tobacco, cigarettes and petroleum products were charged full duty in Aden through which they had to pass on their way inland, and it was intended that the Colony should allow a customs drawback on these re-exported goods to the federations, once they came into existence, thus allowing them to charge their own duties on them without raising prices. As the plan had been approved by the Governor of Aden and the Colonial Office, there was no reason to assume that the Colony would not agree.

The difficulty of getting the states to combine at all was reflected in the care given to the problem of where the Councils of Rulers and Working Committees should meet, for it was recognised that the rulers would be reluctant to meet in one of the state capitals in case it implied that state's pre-eminence. In the case of the Western Federation, the problem could be solved temporarily by meeting in Aden, although it was intended to build a federal capital in due course. The problem was more difficult in the case of the proposed Eastern Federation, which was too distant from Aden to make that town a practicable meeting place. There was therefore no alternative but to propose that the meeting place should be Mukalla, the capital of the Qaiti sultanate, and to hope that jealousy on this point would not obstruct the scheme.

The plan was presented to the rulers at Government House in

January 1954. There were only four absentees: the Haushabi Sultan, who was in the middle of a quarrel with his neighbour the Sultan of Lahej and would not sit with him; Awd bin Saleh, the Upper Aulaqi Sultan, who refused to leave his house at Nisab; the Sultan of Qishn and Socotra, who was far away on the island of Socotra; and the infirm Qaiti Sultan, who had, however, informed his Resident Adviser that he looked with favour on the scheme. Those who attended accepted the project in principle but asked for time to study the details.

After the conference, the Governor of Aden issued a statement which concluded:

> The Rulers and people of these States are entirely free to negotiate among themselves, with such advice of Her Majesty's Government as they may require, such form of association as may suit them best, and which in due course will enable them to benefit by the declared policy of Her Majesty's Government. They shall further have complete freedom among themselves to choose or reject any proposal that may be made for the attainment of the objective of closer association. Her Majesty's Government will afford to any consequent combination of States assistance and protection similar to that which they now afford and will continue to afford to the individual States of the Protectorate.*

The whole aim of the Aden government was to convince the Arab world of the absolute freedom of choice of the rulers. The negotiations with the individual states of the Western Protectorate were conducted in this fashion, though with the reminder that, if a federation came into being, those outside it were likely to be at a disadvantage economically and in respect of British assistance. In retrospect, Sir Tom Hickinbotham concluded that this policy was a mistake and that the hesitant states should have been 'coerced' into joining a federation so that it could have been formed in 1954.†

As it was, the federal scheme came under fierce attack from Yemen and from Egypt, whose radio singled out as traitors and

*Reilly, op. cit., p. 45.
†Hickinbotham, op. cit., p. 169.

infidels those rulers known to be favourable to the scheme. The Arab League naturally supported Yemen, one of its members, and sent a mission under its Secretary General first to Taiz and then to Aden to see the Governor.* This campaign had its effect, for as the months passed the rulers lost heart and the British government, in an effort to demonstrate that no coercion was being used, suspended the negotiations.

After a year in which the Governor of Aden made no move, a few of the Western Protectorate rulers—notably the Sharif of Beihan, who thought the British should not be so mealy-mouthed about forcing states to accept federation—demanded to know what had happened to the plan. Another meeting of the Western Protectorate rulers was held at Government House towards the end of 1955, at which Sir Tom suggested that they should put forward their own plan. But when they failed even to form a Working Committee, they went home.

The proposal for the Eastern Federation crumbled at the very start because of the rivalries of the states. The Wahidi Sultan withdrew his support and proposed joining the Western Federation because he feared his big neighbour, the Qaiti sultanate, and later decided not to join any federation at all. The Kathiri Sultan then decided that he would not link himself with the Qaiti sultanate alone.

III

Throughout 1954 and the first half of 1955, Yemen maintained constant pressure on Protectorate states, giving arms and money to discontented tribal elements and encouraging them to revolt against their rulers. The conference on federation led the Imam to intensify his efforts to upset the frontier states. When the Governor of Aden protested, he replied that federation was a breach of Article 3 of the 1934 treaty. He stirred to rebellion the Dammani subtribe in the Audhali sultanate and the Rabizi in Upper Aulaqi, in an attempt to prevent the building of a road through their territories

*'We had an amusing talk but did not achieve anything worth while'; Hickinbotham, op. cit., p. 169.

45

to Beihan because he believed the road would be pushed through to the potential oilfields at Shabwa. (The British by then knew there was no oil there.) There were twenty-five raids in May 1954, thirty-five in June and forty-two in July.

Having made his point and added to the discouragement of the rulers contemplating federation, the Imam in August invited Sir Tom to visit Taiz, and when the Governor arrived there in October he had friendly discussions, despite the illness from which the Imam was suffering at the time. Verbal agreement was reached about all the current frontier troubles. But when it came to committing the agreement to writing, the Imam revealed that his purpose was to stop the negotiations for federation by demanding that a clause be inserted saying that the 1934 treaty and the 1950 agreements should be honoured and the Governor of Aden conduct himself as his predecessors had done—once more a reference to the Imam's claim that federal proposals were a breach of the 1934 *status quo*. The Governor refused to accept the clause and Yemeni pressure on the Upper Aulaqi tribes intensified.

Imam Ahmed had possibly more confidence in the success of the federal plan than anyone else had. He feared that, once it came into being, the new Shafei state would have an irresistible appeal to the Shafei Muslims who constituted two-thirds of the population of Yemen and had long-standing grievances against Zeidi domination. Through the centuries, they had sought the help of almost any invader in order to secure their independence of the Zeidi hillmen, and they would almost certainly seek the support of their orthodox brethren on the other side of the frontier if the Protectorate Arabs came together in a stable federal state. Imam Ahmed told the Arab League mission that he was in danger of being left—as his forebears had often been—with the mountainous rump of his state and without any access to the sea. It was therefore his policy to keep the Protectorate areas in such a condition of turmoil that social and economic development would be seriously impeded and the advantages of federation diminished.

He sustained his campaign during the first half of 1955, the most serious incident occurring in mid-June when the Shamsi section

of the Rabizi ambushed a government force on its way to the fort at
Rabat, killing two British officers, one Arab officer and five Arab
soldiers. The headman of the Shamsi subtribe was in Yemeni pay.
In the following month a contingent of British troops and Protectorate Levies covered the withdrawal of the small Rabat garrison. Apart
from some minor incidents on the Beihan frontier, the rest of 1955
was quiet—no doubt because word had reached the Imam that the
federal plan was, at least for the time being, moribund.

In October, however, he laid a claim to be ruler of South Arabia
before the Fourth Committee at the UN, when his delegate protested
against Britain's presenting information about Aden. The delegate
said the Colony and the Protectorate were an integral part of Yemen,
'illegally dominated by foreign forces', and contended that Britain
was trying to tighten its hold on the area by its policy of federation
and by bombing innocent tribes. He declared that Yemen had proposed an international fact-finding commission and was still anxious
to reach a settlement by diplomatic means, but if this failed it would
seek a just and equitable settlement through the UN. The British
delegate reiterated that his government had sovereignty over Aden
Colony and responsibility for the external affairs of the Protectorate
states, and 'had no intention of abandoning the obligations which
they have contracted towards the Sultans and other rulers of these
territories'.

During these years of Ahmed's reign, the Foreign Minister, his
brother Prince Seif al-Islam Abdullah, represented the country at
the United Nations and conducted almost all the missions to foreign
countries. He was a man of considerable intelligence and, as his
mind broadened in contact with leading figures of other countries,
he conceived the desire to modernise Yemen to an extent that Imam
Ahmed would never contemplate. With another brother he staged
a *coup d'état* against the Imam in 1955, forcing Ahmed to abdicate
and securing his own election as Imam. Abdullah was too civilised
for the bloody pattern of Yemeni politics and did not kill Ahmed:
a humaneness which the tribes considered a weakness. They rallied
to Ahmed's eldest son, Prince Seif al-Islam Mohammed al-Badr,
who overthrew Abdullah only two days after his election. As soon

as Ahmed was reinstated, he executed Prince Abdullah and his brother, and had pictures of the execution circulated in Aden to discourage Free Yemenis down there. Imam Ahmed concluded from this abortive coup that liberalism, even of the most modest kind, was a weakness he could not afford. He reverted to the harsh, brutal methods of his father.

IV

The political situation in the Arab world in 1956 was very much against the Aden government and those rulers who favoured federation. Notable among the adverse factors was the active support given to Yemeni policy by Saudi Arabia, then in conflict with Britain over the Bureimi oasis which King Saud claimed from the Sultan of Muscat and Oman and the Sheikh of Abu Dhabi, both of whom had British support. King Saud was also the most fervent aide of President Nasser in his opposition to the Baghdad Pact and entered into a defence agreement with Egypt.* Yemen adhered to the agreement in due course. In February 1956, the Saudi government began to intervene actively in the Eastern Protectorate, establishing a base at Sharora, an oasis in Saudi territory, from which truckloads of British and Belgian rifles were sent to Protectorate tribes, mainly the Seiar who owed allegiance to the Qaiti Sultan. Protectorate tribesmen were also invited to the Saudi town of Najran where they were given arms and money. This Saudi intrusion had the full approval of Imam Ahmed, who received $10 million from the Saudi treasury.

The Anglo-French-Israeli invasion of Egypt towards the end of 1956 damaged the British position seriously. Some of the rulers, the die-hards among the merchant class in Aden, and the Indian, Pakistan and Somali minorities, hoped that the intervention would lead to the overthrow of Nasser, although few of them were willing

*The pact, first signed by Iraq and Turkey in January 1955 and eventually joined by Pakistan, Iran and Britain, was bitterly condemned by Nasser, who saw it as an attempt to undermine his influence and restore the British position which had been weakened by the 1954 agreement to withdraw forces from the Suez Canal Zone. Cf. Tom Little, *Modern Egypt*, London 1967.

to say so in public and there were many who disapproved of the method used. The Aden press was also restrained because it represented conservative opinion; but its restraint did not reflect the views of moderates or extremists, who were strongly opposed to the British action and their opinion was shared by many Arab officers in the Government Guards and the Protectorate Levies. These were not the conditions under which plans for federation could be pursued, for the rulers who favoured them felt isolated by the strength of opinion hostile to Britain everywhere in the Arab world.

The execution of Prince Seif al-Islam Abdullah in 1955, the leader of enlightened opinion in the Imam's family and genuinely desirous of better relations with Britain, made the situation worse, for Prince Mohammed al-Badr, Ahmed's son, replaced him as the itinerant exponent of Yemeni policy. He had been educated in Egypt and saw the future of his country as member—however incongruous—of an alliance with Egypt and other progressive states, and he adopted Egypt's policy of non-alignment. This meant in practice that he turned for aid to the Soviet bloc, including (at that time) the People's Republic of China. He made a tour of Eastern Europe, signed a trade and technical agreement with Russia, a commercial agreement with East Germany and an agreement for an exchange of students with Czechoslovakia. In 1957, he made a perfunctory visit to London, but was received with honours in Moscow and Pekin. Prince Mohammed's principal objective was to obtain arms for his own security and to maintain intervention in the Protectorates, and in this he was successful. Contingents of Soviet and Chinese technicians began to arrive in the country and a freighter delivered the first consignment of Soviet arms, ammunition and military equipment to the Yemeni port of Salif, opposite Kamaran Island, in October 1956. (Britain successfully prevented Western powers from supplying arms to Yemen, which compelled Imam Ahmed to agree that his son should look elsewhere.) Diplomatic relations were established with the Soviet Union and People's China, whose ambassadors in Cairo were accredited to Taiz.

Meanwhile the situation in Lahej was far from happy. In 1952, the Sultan had been deposed (he had become homicidally insane)

49

and his younger brother, Ali Abdel Kerim, took over and renewed the treaty of protection with Britain, declaring 'eternal allegiance'. The South Arabian League became more active in the Colony, and when its leader, Mohammed Ali Jifri, went to Cairo in August 1956, the Aden government issued an order excluding him from the Colony. This helped to quieten the situation in Aden, but the brothers of Mohammed Ali, who were influential in Lahej, campaigned there for his return and received the support of the Sultan in doing so.

The trouble in the Colony was partly due to direct incitement by Cairo and Sanaa radios, which openly called on the Adenis to mutiny and violence, and there was also direct intrigue in political and labour affairs which was effective among the workers, many of whom were Yemeni. When Qadhi Mohammed Abdullah al-Shami, Yemeni Minister of State, Governor of Baidha Province and Frontier Affairs Officer, visited Aden for talks with the Sharif of Beihan about frontier matters, he took the opportunity to contact other Protectorate rulers, Aden political leaders and extreme nationalists to further the Yemeni cause and increase the disturbances. Yemen also distributed pamphlets in Aden condemning federation as an imperialist plot and expressing the Imam's strong resentment against Sir Tom Hickinbotham's statement that the Protectorate states were free to decide the future for themselves, which conflicted with Ahmed's claim to sovereignty over them. In March 1956, he reiterated his claim to Kamaran Island because of the suspicion that oil might be found there. (The Aden government had granted exploration rights to the D'Arcy Exploration Company, a subsidiary of British Petroleum.)

Considerable industrial unrest, which manifested itself in March 1956, added to the difficulties. There were thirty strikes involving about 6,000 workers in about five weeks. A commission established in April to inquire into the causes concluded that there were legitimate grievances, and its report led to an improvement of industrial relations—but not before a protracted dock strike did a lot of damage. Inevitably, the industrial troubles were exploited for political ends by the United National Front. It attempted to take control of the movement but had to give way when the unions themselves formed the Aden Trades Union Congress and appointed their own leaders. The Colony had hardly time to recover from this serious situation when the blocking of the Suez Canal in the late autumn of 1956 did further economic damage, for the harbour was almost empty of ships, trade slumped and there were a large number of unemployed. Many of these were Yemenis who went back to their homes, to return later primed for subversion.

Imam Ahmed was convinced that the time had come to mount a major military effort against the Protectorate states. He had the assurance of Russia that he would get arms and ammunition. During 1957, Russian mechanics, military instructors and pilots arrived in Yemen, and about thirty T34 tanks and thirty aircraft, together with anti-aircraft guns, troop transports, lorries, small arms and ammunition, were delivered at Salif, releasing older weapons for distribution to dissident elements in the Protectorates from a base at Baidha. The Yemeni system was to take one hostage in exchange for ten rifles to make sure that the rifles would be used against the rulers and the British and not turned on the Yemenis themselves.

The offensive opened in January 1957 with an attack by Yemeni regular troops on British armoured cars sent to Beihan to defend that state's frontier, which had been under pressure the preceding year. A party of British and American journalists was admitted to Yemen that month; they were entertained at Taiz and Hodeida preliminary to the first press conference ever given by the Imam at Sukhna, the purpose of which was to impress them with the vigour of his resistance to British policy and his unshaken claim to 'South Yemen'. Then they were taken to Qataba to watch the Yemenis launch an attack on the Protectorate but the attack was driven off by Protectorate forces who pursued the Yemenis over the border to Qataba before withdrawing.

There were no less than fifty incidents during February 1957. On February 4, twenty-one Cameron Highlanders on a training patrol were ambushed by Azraqi rebels in the Azraqi tribal area; two were killed and six wounded. Fifteen days later, about a hundred rebel tribesmen, most of them Azraqis, attacked the Dhala Tribal Guard post at Lazariq, capturing five of the guards. At the request of the Dhala Amir, punitive air action was taken against the Azraqis in March, after they had disregarded the usual warnings. Rifles were sent by Yemen to the Ahl Nakhai subtribe in the Fadhli sultanate; and the Sheikh of the Alawi, ruler of a minor state in the Dhala region in treaty relations with Britain, defected to Yemen. Attempts were made to subvert the rulers of Upper and Lower Yafai, and the Protectorate Levies, Government Guards and Tribal Guards in Beihan. Trouble continued sporadically during the year, and was notable for the fact that the Yemeni regulars were now using artillery and heavy machine guns which the British had to silence with shell fire and rockets.

Nevertheless, Imam Ahmed was not happy about having so many foreigners in his country; and when he was warned by the Saudi Arabian government against the Russians, his anxiety about Soviet advisers increased to the point where he asked for permission for Prince Mohammed al-Badr to visit London. Badr was pleased by his reception by the Queen and the Prime Minister in November 1957, but the talks had the opposite effect to that intended by the Imam. Badr made all the usual claims, including the claim to Kamaran Island, and when he found the British attitude as firm as ever, he turned once again to the Eastern bloc. After leaving England, he toured Rumania, Poland, Yugoslavia and China, where he made further requests for military aid.

The British authorities in Aden had trouble with the Lower Yafai sultanate in 1957 owing to the antagonism of Mohammed bin Aidrus, the Naib in the important Abyan plain, which was shared by Lower Yafai and the Fadhli sultanate and was the site of the most notable agricultural and irrigation scheme in the region. The Naib contended that the Aden officials had no right to interfere either in the affairs of the sultanate or of the Abyan Development Board, and his quarrel over this brought him also into conflict with the Lower Yafai State Council. Eventually he took to the hills, and as no one knew exactly where he was or whether or when he was returning, the Yafai members of the Abyan Board brought its work to a halt by refusing to take any decisions. When the Governor of Aden informed the Sultan of Lower Yafai in December that he could not agree to the return of Mohammed bin Aidrus to Abyan, the Naib suddenly reappeared and the Sultan refused to replace him.

The impasse was broken by the Naib's departure once more to his mountain refuge at Al-Qara, but this time he took with him £10,000 from the state treasury and 167 of the 170 Lower Yafai Tribal Guards. While Cairo and Sanaa radio stations glorified his 'noble resistance to colonialism', the Sultan of Lower Yafai tried to enlist the support of the Sultan of Lahej and the South Arabian League on the Naib's behalf, but the State Council stood firm against outside opinion and the Sultan, and appointed a new Naib for Abyan. The Abyan Board subsequently accused Mohammed bin Aidrus of misappropriating considerable sums from its funds. The local administration in Lower Yafai was then reorganised and new Tribal Guards recruited.

The year 1957 drew to a close with the situation more gloomy in Aden and the Protectorates than it had been for very many years, the trouble in Yafai adding its quota to difficulties in Lahej, on the Yemen frontiers and in Aden itself. It was at this point that political developments in the Arab world caused a sharp change in the situation.

V

With the persistence of political instability in Syria, the small but influential and ambitious Ba'ath Socialist Party had sought to achieve power for itself in alliance with the Communist Party. But the communists, by better organisation, had been able to exploit the alliance for their own benefit, and at the end of 1957 were so well established in the high command of the army that they seemed on the threshold of power by a military *coup d'état*. The Ba'athists then took fright and, invoking their first principle of Arab unity, they approached President Nasser to unite Egypt and Syria. In so doing they had for once the support of the conservative President Shukry Kuwatly, who was equally afraid that the communists would seize power. After some hesitation, Nasser agreed and the United Arab Republic came into existence in February 1958 with him as President.

Yemen immediately declared its intention of being associated with the United Arab Republic by an agreement covering political, educational, economic and military affairs, with the armies of all three countries—Egypt, Syria and Yemen—under a single command. Mohammed al-Badr stated in Cairo that he hoped his country's federation with the United Arab Republic 'would lead to the liberation of South Yemen'. It was an incongruous idea that this backward autocratic state should be linked with the two states that considered themselves the vanguard of Arab progress, but Nasser accepted the arrangement and called the new combination the 'United Arab States', to make clear the difference between the complete union of Egypt and Syria and the loose connection with Yemen.

President Nasser regarded Imam Ahmed as typical of the rulers he wanted to remove from power. He calculated that it would eventually be easier to overthrow Ahmed by association with Yemen than from outside. The difference of intention was obvious in their propaganda. Although both Cairo and Sanaa radios attacked the British, Sanaa radio always referred to the Protectorates as 'South Yemen', whereas Cairo referred to them as 'the Arab South', deliberately leaving vague their future relations with Yemen.

Although the connection between Yemen and the UAR never progressed beyond the formation of a joint committee and was virtually still-born, its immediate effect in South Arabia was to make Yemen more attractive to the radicals, most of whom had been unwilling to contemplate union with Yemen because of the reactionary, even brutal, nature of Imam Ahmed's regime. Yemen seemed likely to become an entirely different affair in association with Nasser, who was regarded everywhere as the leader of radical Arab nationalism, and the nationalists of South Arabia were willing to consider union with Yemen if it put them under his banner.* Even

---

*'Tribesmen in the Audhali State adjoining the Yemen can be seen wearing caps nicely embroidered with the device "Long live Gamal" [Abdel Nasser]; and small children in the distant towns of the Hadramaut will dance around the very occasional British visitor, chanting the same slogan'; Nevill Barbour, "Aden and the Arab South", *The World Today*, August 8, 1959.

Mohammed Ali Jifri, the leader of the South Arabian League, whose relations with the Sultan of Lahej were hardly radical and who had always been opposed to union with Yemen, now announced the new policy of his party as 'the liberation of the whole Arab South, natural Yemen, and its inclusion in the UAR.'

Every dissident prince or sheikh in the Protectorates or in exile in Yemen seized on the Yemeni connection with the UAR as a valuable argument. Bruce Condé reported the views of two of them:

Yemen is now federated with the United Arab Republic of Egypt and Syria. It is the wish of the overwhelming majority of the inhabitants of the British-occupied southern parts of Yemen that they, too, be included in the United Arab States Federation, along with the rest of Yemen. . . . In their opinion there is no 'South' separate from Yemen, and no federation save that freely entered into by the will of the Yemenite, Egyptian and Syrian people. . . . The old arguments against union with the mother country 'until reforms have been achieved in Yemen' were no longer valid. Yemen, through technical assistance from European and Asian powers and through UAR federal co-ordination, had begun to improve its internal conditions. Externally, the Imam's government adhered to the liberal Arab policy of independence and unity, which coincided exactly with the desires of the Southern tribes and inhabitants of Aden.*

This new-found enthusiasm made some of the Protectorate rulers afraid that the whole of South Arabia would be swept by the up-surge of feeling into a revolutionary situation which would endanger their own positions even if, as they expected, the union movement eventually came to nothing. They were sure that the Imam's sole object—for he could have no sympathy with either Egyptian or Syrian 'revolutionaries'—was to secure Egyptian help in waging war against the Protectorates. They were proved right when Egyptian and Russian instructors directed Yemeni troops in the use of automatic weapons and artillery, and increased the gravity

*Sheikh Mohammed bin Aidrus of Yafai and Sheikh Saleh Ruwayshan of Al-Baidha, to Bruce Condé, *The Middle East Forum*, No. 8, October 1959.

and number of disturbances on the borders. The reaction of the rulers was entirely the opposite of what Imam Ahmed or President Nasser desired, for it led to the revival of plans for a federation in the Western Protectorate area. The initiative came from the Audhali Sultan, the Sharif of Beihan, and the powerful Naib of the Fadhli sultanate, Ahmed bin Abdullah, who told the Political Agent of the Western Protectorate that they wanted a federation that would eventually become independent but would remain in treaty relationship with Britain.

The Sultan of Lahej, Ali Abdel Kerim, was strongly opposed to the new federal plan because he disliked the leading role taken by Sharif Hussein of Beihan, contending that historically and by right of history he should have primary place in any proposed federal state. He was also influenced by Mohammed Ali Jifri's new policy. During his exile in Egypt, Jifri had been led to believe that, in an independent state of this sort, the Sultan of Lahej, with him as his political aide, would have much better chance of leadership than the reactionary Zeidi ruling family of Yemen. The Sultan did not declare publicly his support for Jifri, but he allowed him to make Lahej the base for South Arabian League subversion and to issue from there pamphlets calling on 'true Arabs' to kill the British advisory staff and on Government Guards to revolt.

In April 1958, the British Adviser in Lahej tried to arrest and deport the three Jifri brothers, but his party of Government Guards and British troops was able only to take Abdullah, the Director of Education, as Mohammed Ali was in Yemen and Alawi in Upper Aulaqi territory. This high-handed action and the Governor's order stationing Guards in Lahej incensed the Sultan who first protested to Aden and then left for London, ostensibly to get medical treatment for the Sultana, but really to protest to the Colonial Secretary.

Strong action by the Governor had been made necessary by the increasing number of incidents in the colony, which was manifest in March by the number of bomb and grenade explosions; a British officer was killed by a grenade thrown onto his bed while he was asleep. The troubles continued in April, and on May 2 a State of Emergency was declared. When it was established that some of the terrorism was instigated by Mohammed bin Aidrus, who was sending hand grenades and time-bombs from Al-Qara, the RAF destroyed his house there and with it most of his money and ammunition. One of the men arrested in Aden in possession of Russian and German explosives confessed that he had received them from Mohammed Ali Jifri. There was no proof that Yemen was directly involved, although there was little doubt that Jifri and Aidrus bought or were given the explosives in Taiz.

Yemen was actively involved in troubles in Dhala in April. This was one of the states in which the right of the Amir to rule was disputed within the family by the ex-Regent Haidara who had been expelled by the British some years earlier for alleged malpractices. Haidara was residing in the Yemeni town of Qataba, just over the frontier, and as he was strong and the Amir Shaaful weak he was still feared in the amirate and the Radfan country nearby. Yemen supported him in organising a revolt of Dhala tribes for the purpose of detaching the Jabal Jihaf from the amirate, and supplied a large number of rifles to the Jihafi, Azraqi, Humaidi and Shairi tribes in exchange for hostages. Led by the Yemeni Governor of Qataba, several hundred of these tribesmen converged on the Jihaf mountain, Haidara established himself at Al-Ruqaba, and a Yemeni official distributed money and ammunition among the villages. The Assistant British Adviser who went to al-Sarir fort to investigate the Jabal Jihafi situation was besieged by this large force; though one company of Protectorate Levies broke through to him, two other attempts to relieve the fort failed. It took a major engagement by two companies of the Shropshire Light Infantry, supported by Levies and by the RAF, to raise the siege. The rebel tribesmen fled over the frontier into Yemen, and the RAF destroyed Qataba barracks and Yemeni machine-gun posts which had been firing over the border.

This serious incident was hardly over when Yahya Harsi, commandant of the Lahej regular forces, deserted to Taiz with two-thirds of his army and Government Guards and £10,000 from the state treasury. Convinced that he had done so on the orders of Sultan Ali Abdel Kerim, who was known to be in contact with the Imam, the British withdrew their recognition of him as Sultan, and the

Council of Electors appointed his cousin, Amir Fadhl bin Ali
as acting head of state. In December 1958, the Council deposed
Sultan Ali and confirmed Amir Fadhl as ruler, and he was recognised by the British government. Yahya Harsi tried to raise the
Subeihi tribes, who were potentially good material for revolt
because their territory had been incorporated in Lahej originally
against their will; but most of them took his letters, inviting them to
Taiz to plan the rebellion, to the British. Ali Abdel Kerim went from
London to Cairo where he became a leading propagandist against
the Aden government;* but a visit he paid in September to Imam
Ahmed failed to achieve anything because he rejected the Imam's
claim to rule the Protectorate.

The situation was inopportune for the efforts of both Harsi and
Sultan Ali because Imam Ahmed had changed his policy after the
Dhala affair and had decided to try to talk the British into abandoning the federation project. To that end he kept the frontier quiet in
the latter half of 1958, and most of the dissident Dhala tribesmen
and the Lahej soldiers returned to their homes. The British Chargé
d'Affaires in Taiz made contact with the Yemeni government in
response to a proposal it had made to discuss the frontier situation in
January but which had lain in abeyance during the troubled months.
Two officials from each side met in July 1958 in the Emperor of
Ethiopia's palace at Diredawa which he offered for the purpose, but
the talks about a cease-fire and the return of dissidents were as
usual inconclusive. Nevertheless, the Imam, in pursuit of his aim
to stop the federal project, did not resume fighting on the frontier.

Even as the talks at Diredawa were in progress the final touches
were being put to the federal project. In June the Amir of Dhala,
spurred by his own troubles, had asked to join the proposed federation and the Sheikh of Upper Aulaqi followed suit. Together with
the original three main proponents of the project—the rulers of
Audhali and Beihan, and the Naib of the Fadhli sultanate—they
visited London to discuss federation with the Minister of State

*'. . . the intense dislike which Arab nationalists feel towards the systems of
little princedoms much reduces whatever effect his appeals might otherwise
have'; Nevill Barbour, op. cit.

for the Colonies. On July 16, the British government announced its agreement in principle with the proposal of the five states to federate and offered to support it. At this, the Sultan of Lower Yafai agreed to join, and the six founder states met with the Governor of Aden to discuss a draft constitution, which had already been prepared.

VI

The inauguration of the Federation of the Amirates of the South took place in Aden on February 11, 1959, in the presence of the rulers or deputies (Naibs) of the six founder states*, Lennox-Boyd, the Colonial Secretary, and Sir William Luce, Governor of Aden (who had replaced Sir Tom Hickinbotham in 1956). Sultan Ahmed bin Abdullah, OBE, Naib of the Fahdli state, spoke for the federating rulers†, welcoming the Federation and the treaty with Britain, which was signed immediately after the constitution. Lennox-Boyd reaffirmed Britain's continuing ties of friendship with the amirates:

> This Federation poses a threat to no one and no country. It has come into existence by the will of the people acting through their traditional tribal leaders and it has come into existence so that together the Amirates of this territory can give expression to their desire to pool their resources, to live without fear of subversion or attack, and to give their people greater security and prosperity‡.

The constitution provided for a Council of Six Ministers with executive authority, the chairmanship of which would rotate monthly among the members, and a Federal Council with legislative authority

*The Dhala amirate, the Audhali sultanate, the Upper Aulaqi sheikhdom, the Beihan amirate, the Fadhli sultanate and the Lower Yafai sultanate. The Dathina confederation, the Lower Aulaqi, Haushabi and Lahej sultanates had all asked to join the Federation before the ceremony, but arrangements for them were not completed until much later.

†'In the absence of the Fadhli Sultan, Abdullah bin Uthman, who bitterly opposed his State's inclusion in the grouping'; Sheikh Mohammed bin Aidrus of Yafai and Sheikh Saleh Ruwayshan of Al-Baidha, to Bruce Condé, op. cit. As mentioned earlier, these two Sheikhs were dissident leaders in exile in Yemen.

‡Reuter's report.

consisting of six members nominated from each of the states. The British treaty with the Federation followed the pattern of the protecting and advisory treaties with the individual states, the British government taking responsibility for external affairs and protection, and the federal government undertaking not to enter into any treaty, agreement or correspondence or other relations with any foreign state or government or international organisation without the knowledge and consent of the British. The Federation also agreed to be bound to accept British advice on any matter connected with the good government of their territories. Britain, for its part, committed itself to financial aid for social, economic and political development and for the maintenance of a Federal Army and National Guard. The Government Guards of the Western Protectorate area were subsequently transferred to the Federation and became the nucleus of its National Guard.

The British government was pleased to have the Federation at last, as the financial terms of the treaty demonstrated. The idea expressed by Sir Tom Hickinbotham that federation was one way of keeping down costs, and therefore the charge on the British taxpayer, had clearly been abandoned, for the aid offered to the Federation was going to cost more. This proved to be the case. Before the Second World War, Britain's contribution to the Protectorate states was £100,000 per annum. In 1954, it was £800,000, but in no time at all Britain's assistance to the Federation amounted to £5 million: an increase vastly in excess of the change in money values. Sir William Luce had prepared the way for this change during a visit to London in 1957, when he made it clear to the government that the Federation was a non-starter unless more money was available for the backward states. The possibility that oil would be discovered in the Eastern Protectorate area was responsible for the additional emphasis put on money by the Western states, in which oil prospecting had proved a failure. (The belief that they would become oil-producing countries reinforced the Eastern states' decision not to join a federation because they saw themselves becoming rich enough to buy their own defences or buy off their enemies.)

Sir William's persuasion was not, however, the only reason for Britain's generosity. The loss of the British base in Egypt, the failure of the Suez invasion in 1956, and uncertainty about the bases in Cyprus and in Kenya, had greatly heightened the importance of Aden as the centre from which Britain's interests in the Persian Gulf and responsibilities further East could be safeguarded. The situation in the Middle East as a whole was far from happy as a result of the revolutionary momentum that followed the union of Syria and Egypt in 1958 and the greatly enhanced status of President Nasser. Because of his overt enmity to Nasser and the union, King Saud had been compelled to hand over responsibility for his kingdom to the Prime Minister, his brother Prince Feisal. Civil war in Lebanon and an abortive *coup-d'état* in Jordan had demonstrated the vulnerability of these two pro-Western states. Above all, in Iraq the royal family and their powerful henchman, Nuri al-Said, had been murdered and an anti-Western republic established. Although by the time the Federation came into existence the revolutionary tide had begun to subside because of troubles in the United Arab Republic, Prince Feisal's wariness with regard to Nasser, and the survival of King Hussein of Jordan, the events of 1958 had revealed in no uncertain fashion the dangers facing Britain. They pointed, so the British government concluded, to the clear need for the base in Aden and—reverting to the very origin of British policy in the hinterland—the equal need for a buffer area offering protection to the base. The Federation seemed to offer the best form of buffer, for it was likely that it could make a better show of defence against Yemen and any other outside intervention than could a number of small, bickering and separate states.

Nor was it possible for the British government to ignore the activities of Russia, which was spending far more in the provision of arms to Yemen than in practical development aid. The idea of Khrushchev presenting himself as defender of the free against wicked British imperialism, extending his podgy paw of friendship to that antique denial of all liberties, the Imam of Yemen, was so cynical an absurdity that there was bound to be a more real motive for it. The motive might only be to make life more difficult for the British and hasten their departure by the supply of more effective artillery and automatic weapons, but there could be the long-term objective of turning Yemen into a satellite. This was not a prospect that could be regarded with any equanimity, for Aden was equalling New York and Singapore as a bunkering port and was vital for fuelling ships on the Asian and African routes from the Mediterranean. Further, the Straits of Mandeb were the southern gate of the Red Sea just as the Suez Canal was the northern, and with the Soviet position in Egypt strengthening daily, it seemed wise to hold the Straits.

VII

Parallel with the problem of the Protectorate area was the condition of Aden itself, for it was deeply, if confusedly, affected by the strong tides of radical opinion sweeping the Middle East and was not likely to accept much longer the colonial form of administration which offered the people virtually no say in their affairs. There was not much point in having a buffer area behind Aden if the Colony itself was wrecked by internal disorder. Sir William Luce's second theme during his discussions in London in 1957 was, therefore, the need to make constitutional advances in Aden, and this in effect meant giving the people a majority of elected members to the Legislative Council. These proposals were contained in a *Gazette Extraordinary* published on November 11, 1957, which announced that the un-official elected members of the Council would for the first time have a majority of twelve against five ex-officio official members and six nominated members. This decision was taken despite the fact that, in earlier elections to the Municipal Committee of Aden, seven of the fourteen elected members were radical nationalists, which indi-cated that the radical movement had gained considerable ground.

The decision was a wise one and, if it erred, the error was on the side of too much timidity. The response of Aden to the propaganda which had deluged it over recent years was more sophisticated than one might have expected, and there was no reason to assume that the national movement could not share the rational evolution of the Colony. At this stage of development there were few Adenis who desired union with Yemen, who related their admiration for Gamal Abdel Nasser into a design to put themselves into his charge, or who were willing to sacrifice the prosperity of the Colony for an uncertain political future. Broadly speaking, they desired to be able to hold their head high as independent people, and most of them had little sympathy for discontented princes in the Protectorate areas who rebelled against their rulers for the simple purpose of replacing them. Ideas about what particular form the advance should take, and how fast it should come about, varied almost from person to person, and even within the various political organisations. But their opposition to the British was rooted in a belief that Britain was not imposing more changes on the tribal areas and not giving sufficient economic aid to help the tribesmen into the modern world. Their attitude towards the Aden government was 'bolshie' in the colloquial sense but not revolutionary. Communists had no hold on Aden or the Protectorates, and their attempts to distribute pamphlets in the Colony met with no response.

The new constitution came into force in January 1959. There was no change, however, in the much-disputed franchise under which no one could vote unless he was born in Aden, or was a British subject or a British-protected subject who had lived in the colony for seven out of the last ten years. The process of constitutional change and the transfer of responsibilities had been described as Adenisation, but the question of who constituted an Adeni was so complicated that a committee had to be formed to try to define him. When Britain occupied Aden in 1839, the population was about 500; in 1959 it was nearly 140,000, a great number of whom were immigrants or descendants of immigrants from the Indian subcontinent or from British Somaliland, and they were entitled to vote. But one third of the population were Yemenis, the vast majority of whom had no right to vote. It is true that many of the Yemenis travelled in and out of Aden, but a large proportion of them could certainly have qualified on the seven-year rule; and they were Arabs, whereas the Indians and Somalis were not and were, into the bargain, unpopular.

The Yemenis were, in the main, people who had escaped from the tyranny of their own country, but the association of Yemen with the United Arab Republic inspired their patriotism and gave them hope. They constituted, furthermore, a substantial proportion of the Aden trade unionists who provided the mass of radical nationalists. Although the Aden government was anxious to reform the franchise, it had no desire to have the elections dominated by these people who could be marshalled by extremist leaders. The leaders of the now powerful Aden Trades Union Congress (ATUC) were anxious to have them enfranchised for the obvious reason that their votes would give them a dominant electoral position; when they were denied the right to vote, the ATUC called for a boycott of the elections. In this they were supported by Radio Cairo. The boycott was most successful in Little Aden, where most of the potential voters were workers, and only 15 per cent of the electorate there went to the polls; but in the main Arab area of Crater the vote was 43 per cent. The successful candidates were mostly from the Aden Association and other moderates, with the result that the Legislative Council broadly represented Aden for the Adenese and the orderly development of self-government.

The relations between Aden and the Federation had been a subject of discussion among British officials ever since the idea was conceived, and Sir Tom Hickinbotham was on record as saying that he believed they should ultimately unite in one state.* It was difficult to see how they could remain forever separate, for they were closely linked in many ways other than the fact that they both came under the same Governor. Aden was the gateway to the Federation, through which all means of communication passed; it provided the Arab personnel for administration and development in the Federation; and it was in or near Aden that the capital of the Federation had to be established to avoid tribal rivalries. Perhaps with a great deal of money and in the passage of time, this dependence on the Colony could be reduced by creating a new port, by training personnel and overcoming rivalries; but for most people it hardly seemed sensible to go to all this trouble and cost when all the facilities existed ready-made in Aden. Nor was the dependence one-sided. Aden was so minute that even the road linking Aden with Little Aden was

*Hickinbotham, op. cit., p. 171.

virtually a frontier with the Federation; without the British it was defenceless before the tribes. It obtained from the federal area its water, most of its fruit and vegetables, and a high proportion of its labour force. Without union, the Federation was a country without a commercial and administrative capital, and Aden was a capital without a country.

Some British officials, however, considered that the difficulty of union outweighed the advantage, and held that Britain's purpose in South Arabia could be best served by keeping firmly to the original concept of a buffer area behind and separate from the Colony. They did not want the tribal areas caught in the tangle of Aden politics. An influential section of the Aden population was on their side, although for different reasons: they feared that the wealth of the port would be used to subsidise the tribal areas and that to some extent they would come under the authority of tribal rulers and depend for their security on tribal forces. On the other hand, it was obvious that Aden could not remain a colony indefinitely while Arab nationalism was everywhere else on the march, and many of the Arab officials and politicians saw their future as an independent state within the Federation. Every shade of radical opinion advocating one or other kind of independent South Arabia was in favour of Aden's union with its hinterland, even though they opposed the British way of going about it and suspected British objectives. Their suspicions were correct to the extent that the British government had no intention of sacrificing its control of Aden, which was now required for military as well as maritime purposes. This was the fly in the ointment. Those working with the Aden government and those opposing it were both agreed that Aden should eventually be independent enough to decide its own future and its relations with the tribal areas and even Yemen. They differed mainly about timing and trust in the British.

Even so, the Federation was making steady progress. In October 1959 Lahej joined—an important step, for it brought into the fold the largest state in the Western Protectorate and no less than a quarter of the total population of the area. In the preceding month the foundation stone of the federal capital, Al-Ittihad (Union) was laid just outside Aden on a piece of land leased from the Aqrabi state. (The Council was meanwhile meeting in the tiny enclave of Bir Ahmed, between the Colony and Lahej.) Early in 1960, the Lower Aulaqi sultanate, the Dathina confederation and the Aqrabi sheikdom became members. Thus, there were ten states in the Federation.

Informal discussions to bring in Aden were now under way between the British officials and leading Adenis. At this point, the governorate of Sir William Luce, a distinguished administrator with long service in the Sudan, came to a close. He had worked with an assistant from the Foreign Office, Horace Phillips. Perhaps to signify the changing situation, Sir William was replaced by Sir Charles Johnston, a Foreign Office official whose last post had been Ambassador in Amman.

In January 1961, Sir Charles told the Legislative Council that the British government agreed to the introduction of a ministerial system of government. This change had little practical meaning, since it simply confirmed Arabs in charge of departments of government, but it had psychological importance. It did not meet the demands of the Council, which had asked five months earlier for a new constitution to be brought into effect before the end of 1962. The governor replied indirectly to this request when he said that he was pursuing the question as speedily as possible but he asked them 'to be patient'. He added that it would be some time before the government would be in a position to announce firm proposals because there were many complex problems involved, including the 'possibility of closer association with the Western Aden Protectorate and in particular with the Arab Amirates of the South'. Sir Charles had, in fact, made up his own mind 'that constitutional advance in Aden was essential, but that it must not only be unmistakably intended as an approach to merger, but must also be so designed as to facilitate the merger process and to minimise the risk of it going wrong'. As he saw it, the problem existed in the priorities: constitutional advance in Aden first, or merger first.* Whether they knew it or not, the members of the Legislative Council were committed to a policy about which the only doubt was as to the method of its

*Sir Charles Hepburn Johnston, *The View from Steamer Point*, 1964, p. 37.

execution. As a first step to resolving the problem, Sir Charles suggested to London that there should be three-sided discussions among the British government, representatives of the Federation and those of Aden. This advice was accepted, and in April 1961 the Colonial Secretary, Iain Macleod, visited the Colony for discussions with local leaders which set the stage for conference.

There had been ominous signs by 1960 of the form of difficulty Aden was going to face in the future. In the early part of that year there were a number of strikes, notably one at the BP refinery which lasted for ten weeks. This disruption of trade on which Aden totally depended was a serious threat to its future, even more so because the political undertone of the strikes made them different from the earlier ones which had definite grievances to eradicate. Sir William Luce called in experts to advise on the situation, and on the strength of their report he framed an Industrial Relations Ordinance which Hassan al-Bayoomi, the strong-willed Minister of Labour, steered through the Legislative Council despite a series of one-hour protest strikes organised by the ATUC.

The ordinance in effect banned strikes by imposing prior processes of conciliation through which claims had to pass, and it established an Industrial Court to settle disputes concerning workers. Although the International Confederation of Free Trade Unions and the British Trades Union Congress protested against this 'repressive' measure, it was more liberal than any trade-union law in the Arab world, where strikes were almost everywhere totally prohibited. It had the required effect in Aden for a considerable time by halting the epidemic of damaging strikes, but its long-term political effect was damaging to over-all policy by destroying what little chance there was of unions compromising with the government. In particular, it strengthened antagonism towards Bayoomi; this was to be important because he became the principal architect of federation on the Aden side.

4

The Aden Merger

IF AN independent state of South Arabia were to exist at all, it
seemed essential that Aden and the tribal areas, which were so
dependent on each other despite their disparity, should be joined
together. Yet it took nearly twenty months of discussion and a good
deal of persuasion by the Governor of Aden and the British government to bring the union about. These discussions were conducted
under the threat of what the Governor called 'the ticking time-
bomb'—the date in January 1963 when the term of the existing
Legislative Council was due to end—but such were the hazards
and uncertainties in the case that he was compelled in the end to
defuse the bomb by prolonging the Council's term by decree.

Not the least of the difficulties was the demand of a majority of
Adenis, including many who were considered moderate, that Aden
should not be committed to the union by a Legislative Council which
had come into being in 1959 on a 27 per cent vote without any
mandate to make so dramatic a change in their political and domestic condition. This legitimate argument suffered from two serious
defects. In the first place, no one had yet agreed on an acceptable
franchise by which a new Council could be elected. Secondly, a
franchise acceptable to the majority would certainly produce a
Council that would reject any federation under British auspices,
for there were strong factions which contended that Aden should be
completely independent of the British before it was called on to
decide its connection or lack of connection with the tribal areas or,
for that matter, with Yemen. The Governor had decided on union,

the British government had agreed to union, the majority of the ministers in the Aden government wanted union, but it was bound to be what David Holden called a 'shotgun wedding'.*

I

The process was facilitated by the inability of the critics of the proposed merger to make common cause against the Aden government and the British, for there were as yet only factions instead of parties, and the most powerful mass movement, the Trades Union Congress, still lacked political leadership. Even the Aden Association, which had been formed in 1949 and had once had enough influence to speak directly to the Minister of State for the Colonies, had split in 1958 over an extraneous issue that showed how fragile were political alliances—whether the mild narcotic *qat* should be banned from the Colony.† Over this issue Mohammed Ali Luqman, the lawyer and newspaper proprietor and first 'ideologist' of Adeni nationalism, parted company with the much more formidable political leader Hassan Ali Bayoomi who had become the most effective Adeni minister in the government.

In 1960, Luqman tried to revive the Association and establish branches all over the Colony, starting first in the oil town of Little Aden which was considered by the BP Refinery Union to be its preserve. This embittered relations between the Association and the Aden TUC, which were never good; the Congress condemned the Association as 'a separationist movement, anti-mother Yemen, anti-Arab nationalism . . .'. There was not much difference between the factions of Luqman and Bayoomi on the question of federation,

---

*David Holden, *Farewell to Arabia*, 1966, p. 56.

†The Adenis are great chewers of *qat*, but the dispute was not about its damage to health, which is perhaps no greater than that of alcohol. About £2,500,000-worth was consumed yearly in the colony, almost all of which was imported from either Yemen or Ethiopia. The Aden Association, arguing that this was a dreadful waste, successfully got the ban imposed. Like most bans of this sort it was not a success and Hassan Ali Bayoomi, himself a chewer of *qat*, successfully campaigned for the removal of the ban in face of bitter opposition from Mohammed Ali Luqman.

69

however, for neither demanded full independence of Britain as a precondition; both wanted complete self-government as a colony before federation. But, whereas Luqman stood strictly by the demand, Bayoomi was flexible in his approach. Both held the view that any independent South Arabian state of which Aden became a part should be a republic, that is, not under the British Crown, the Yemeni Imam or the Sultan of Lahej.

This objection to any form of monarchical sovereignty cut them off from all other movements. Whatever lip-service was given by the South Arabian League to the United Arab States, its real objective was still a South Arabian federation excluding Yemen and under the sovereignty of the former Sultan of Lahej, Ali Abdel Kerim. But the League was equally in decay because its three leaders, Mohammed Ali Jifri, Sheikhan Abdullah al-Habshi and Qahtan Mohammed as-Shaabi, were all in exile in Cairo with the deposed Sultan, who no longer had enough funds to support the movement in Aden. The United National Front, which was formed in 1955 as a splinter of the League, was to all intents and purposes a political wing of the Aden TUC and had adequate funds from Yemen. It opposed strongly both the League and the Association as 'separationist' and demanded union with Yemen. The Front had also fallen on bad times by the time the merger became practical politics owing to quarrels among the leaders over 'misuse' of the money from Yemen.

Mohammed Ali Luqman called his new organisation rather grandly the People's Constitutional Congress, but it was no more than the ineffective rump of the Aden Association. There were also numerous political groups or clubs which mushroomed around the federal debate, eighteen of which collaborated under the name of the so-called National Congress, which was pro-Yemen. Apart from the National Congress and the ATUC, all the political parties or groups were prepared to accept some form of federation and to that extent were not in headlong collision with the government or Britain. But they were also unanimous in wanting a 'national government' for the Colony which could meet the federal rulers as master in its own house.

Neither the British government nor the Governor had, therefore, any reason to fear organised opposition, apart from industrial action by the unions, but this did not mean that opposition and doubt were non-existent even in moderate quarters. There was, in the first place, the economic disparity between the Colony and the Federation. The area of the latter was for the most part mountainous and barren, with 90 per cent of the people eking out a precarious living by cultivating the one per cent of land fit for agriculture, or by weaving, fishing or preparing hides and skins. The remaining 10 per cent were nomads roaming a wilderness through which there were only the most primitive communications. The Colony, on the other hand, was a thriving port with a valuable entrepôt trade and a very important and growing income from the British military and air base. Aden was now one of Britain's major strategic centres and these bases contributed in one form or another about £11 million a year to the Colony. In contrast, the £1,400,000 spent by Britain to develop the tribal area was considered totally inadequate by many thinking people. The president of the Aden Chamber of Commerce, A. B. Besse, head of a commercial 'empire' in South Arabia and the Horn of Africa, and himself born in Aden, told the Chamber in his annual address for 1961 that 'it seems unlikely that the Colony will contemplate a closer link until the Protectorates are economically more advanced'. This view that union was desirable but needed a great deal of time and money to make it worthwhile was shared by most of the trading fraternity.

The ordinary citizen of Aden feared that any form of association with the Protectorate states would make him subject to 'feudal' sheikhs who would be supported by the British and able to enforce their rule by a well-equipped and trained army formed of their tribesmen—for that in effect was how he viewed the transfer of the Levies and Guards to the Federation. The Adenis themselves had no military training and did not want their security dependent on tribal troops. Occasional incidents heightened their fears, as when an Arab commander of a Government Guard unit raided an Aden police station with submachine guns to free one of his men who had been detained by the police for questioning about an offence against a woman. Although they found many grounds for criticising the colonial administration, when faced with the Federation the Adenis began to measure its virtues against the absence of them outside. These inhabitants of a colony, with all the limitations of colonial status this entailed, were above all concerned with the preservation of the human rights they enjoyed even as subject people and might lose if the British protection were removed. Their democracy might be in its infancy but they wanted to be sure it would live and grow; that their judicial system with its right of appeal to the Privy Council would not be tampered with; that conditions of work in the civil service would not be changed except for the better; that progress in both health and education services would be maintained; and that workers' rights and the trade unions would not be left to the mercy of tribal leaders who knew little about them and disliked what they knew.

For the mass of simple people in South Arabia, federal plans and the discussions about them were in any case meaningless.

As for the ordinary Adeni, the man in the street, these talks mean nothing to him. He would rather continue to live as happily as his grandfathers did ever since Britain took this fortress over from the Sultan of Lahej more than 120 years ago. The same applies to the ordinary Protectorate man, with perhaps one difference—that he does not need anybody's protection or interference: he is content with his way of life and is capable of looking after himself.*

The Yemenis in the Colony looked with considerable anxiety on the developing situation, particularly with regard to the constitutional changes that were expected to precede or occur with federation, for this substantial section of the population were in many respects second-class citizens. Although many of them had lived in Aden for forty years or more, they were still Yemenis; to have taken out naturalisation papers would have cut them off from their families in the home country and have laid them open to the danger of execution if they returned themselves, so strong was the opposition of the Imam. This put them at a disadvantage in arguing their case.

*Mohammed Ahmed Barakat, a journalist, in a letter to the author dated August 10, 1961.

It was further damaged by those Yemenis who, overtly or subversively, were active in the Imam's cause and thereby brought the whole community under suspicion.

Apart from lacking any political rights, the Yemenis as aliens were debarred from the government service and from many firms engaged on government work. They could not get automatic 'exemption permits' which enabled them to leave and re-enter the colony. They could have education for the Aden-born child but not for a child born in Yemen, and they could very readily be deported. Adeni sympathy for them was relative. The average Adeni certainly felt more warmly disposed to the Yemeni in Aden than to the British subject from the Commonwealth countries or to the Somali who by seven years' residence could acquire all the rights, facilities and opportunities of the colony—an advantage which the Adenis had always resented. But this did not make them willing to give the Yemenis equal political rights. A proposal to do so was rejected by the Legislative Council in 1959 without much encouragement from the British.

The leaders of the Yemeni community advocated that an Adeni should be any Arab whose mother tongue was Arabic and had been born of Arab parents in Aden, or an Arab born in the Protectorate area or in Yemen whose mother tongue was Arabic and who had resided in Aden for seven years: any person thus qualified should have political rights and be entitled to join the public service. It was hardly likely that any British government or administration would accept this definition, which would have disenfranchised thousands of Aden-born Commonwealth citizens and Somalis, most of whom had no other home but Aden and some of whom held high and influential posts in the administration. Because their concept of Adeni identity was unacceptable to the British and the influential Indian group, the Yemenis' hope lay in the creation of an independent Aden state whose nationality they could adopt without being condemned as infidels by the Imam. But they had nothing to gain by internal self-government approved by the strict Adeni movement as prelude to a federation which might put their status wholly or in part at the disposal of tribal rulers totally opposed to Yemen. This being the case, the Yemenis, who were more than a third of the population of the Colony, were opposed to the federal plan and to the constitutional development being carried out by the British and the existing Aden government.

The Governor and the British government were able to generalise that 'most people wanted federation' only by ignoring the conditions that most people attached to it; yet it was possibly true that no action could have been taken by them if they had attempted to act in accordance with a public opinion so complex that a consensus was impossible. They therefore disregarded it until it caused trouble, and concerned themselves only with public opinion as it was interpreted by those people with whom they had to deal: the Aden ministers and the federal rulers. As Sir Charles Johnston later wrote: '. . . it was only possible to conclude that the best solution for all concerned would be a merger of the Colony and the Federation in a single unit, having a special relationship with Britain which would ensure us the retention of our strategic facilities for as long as we needed them.'*

The federal rulers did not concern themselves about opinion but only with the consummation of the merger on terms acceptable to themselves; but this was not the case with the Aden ministers, whose attitudes covered a broad spectrum of moderate local opinion. Bayoomi's group was willing to bargain its way through to union as rapidly as possible, but Abdullah Saidi, who belonged to the Luqman political faction, was more concerned with the difficulties likely to beset Aden if it joined. The moderation of Ali Salem Ali, a left-wing independent, was little more than a veneer that was likely to peel-off in the heat of debate.

The two issues likely to test the ministers and the rulers when it came down to detail were the status of Aden in the Federation and the economics of it. Aden felt it had a right to enter as an equal to the existing Federation of the amirates because of its greater wealth, social advancement and key position; but the more extreme opinion among the rulers held that it should enter as just one more state, with no more representation in the Supreme Council or other organs

*Johnston, op. cit., p. 36.

74

of government than any other state. The economics of the union constituted a highly sensitive subject to the Aden ministers, who shared the popular view that the Colony could lose heavily, but this was more a matter for expert study than of principle. Finally, there were the issues common to all federal schemes: the balance between federal and local responsibilities, and the structure and control of the civil service.

The conference in London in June and July 1961 did not deal in detail with any of these problems. Iain Macleod received the federal ministers and G. K. N. Trevaskis first and they were joined later by the Aden ministers and the Governor. It was agreed that they would push forward both with the constitutional developments in Aden and the proposed merger. The timetable to be aimed at was the conclusion of detailed plans in Aden before October, so that the whole scheme could be completed at another conference in London before the end of the year. However, when the discussions were resumed at Government House in Aden in August, it was quickly apparent that the timetable was unrealistic, for the placid air of the London generalisations vanished in the heat of detailed debate between the ministers and the rulers and among the ministers themselves. Joint working parties were established, however, to consider those departments which had already become a federal responsibility for the amirates and which should be federal if Aden joined.

In October 1961, when the plan should have been reaching completion, Ali Salem Ali resigned on the pretext that his father's illness compelled him to concentrate on the family business and he became a strong opponent of federation in the form it seemed likely to take. The British government meanwhile sent out Sir Richard Ramage to advise on the civil service and Mr Pearl on finance. With their help and the help of British experts in Aden, solutions were found to both problems. It was agreed that, in order to preserve the cadre of British civil servants, the British government would put them at the disposal of the Governor who would then make those who were needed available to the federal or Aden governments; that the Aden Public Service Commission would remain in advisory relationship to the Governor to protect the service against partiality and nepotism, and that a similar commission would be established in the Federation in an advisory capacity to the Supreme Council, with the proviso that, in the cases of Aden civil servants transferred to the Federation, the Supreme Council would defer to the Governor. The pattern of agreement on finance, designed to ensure that Aden did not lose by the deal, was that the cost of Aden departments transferred to the Federation should be met from those Aden revenues, such as customs, that would also be transferred. Customs were to become a federal subject and the individual states would be compensated for any loss of customs revenues.

Many months had passed and the next date for reporting to London—May 1962—had already arrived without any agreement on the degree of Aden's representation in the Federation. At last, however, the two sides reached a compromise by which Aden would have four ministers out of fourteen on the Supreme Council and twenty-four out of eighty-five on the Federal Council. With this agreement, the Governor was able to report to the Secretary of State for the Colonies that the next conference in London could take place in July. At this point Abdullah Saidi, of the People's Constitutional Congress (the Luqman group), refused to sign the agreement on the grounds that elections should be held in Aden before going any further. As in the case of Ali Salem Ali, the Governor appointed a more tractable member of the Legislative Council in his place.

On the grounds that the plan must be approved by the British government, the terms of the agreement were not announced in Aden, and Abdullah Saidi was warned that under the Secrets Ordinance he had also to keep silent.* Even so, a great deal was already known of the discussions, and, despite the opinion held in Government House that the Adenis had come to accept the merger idea, there was a great deal of discontent not far below the surface. This was particularly manifest over the question of the elections due to take place in January 1963, because it was known or guessed that the constitutional changes in Aden would take place in the

*Saidi died of heart failure in London in the autumn.

autumn and that the elections would be postponed until federation was a fact.

The military support given by the British to Kuwait when it was threatened with invasion by Iraq in July 1961 had convinced London more than ever of the need to retain the Aden base, and when the conference reassembled in London in July 1962, the new Colonial Secretary, Duncan Sandys, was all for pushing through the merger as fast as possible with an agreement which would enable Britain to keep this base. This made it inevitable that the elections would be postponed, but even the Aden ministers who agreed that postponement could not be avoided were not happy that so important a matter as the merger should be decided by the Governor's Executive Council on which sat no less than four British ex-officio members.

It had been agreed in the Aden talks that the Governor—to be called the High Commissioner—would keep responsibility for external affairs, defence and security when the merger took place, and that some time in advance of the merger the Executive Council would be transformed into a Council of Ministers which would consist entirely of ministers drawn from the elected members of the Legislative Council and would exclude all ex-officio members, except the Attorney General, from the Executive and the Legislature. The Aden ministers wanted the federal plan resubmitted to the reformed Council when it came into existence, whereas the federal ministers strongly opposed doing so because they feared there would be many more months of discussion, with old points raised again, before the scheme could go through. Eventually both sides accepted a British compromise which provided that the Legislative Council would elect the four new members who would sit alongside the four ex-officio members until the federal union took place, when the ex-officio members would withdraw. As the merger could not possibly be effected in the remaining time available before the scheduled election date, it followed that the constitutional change had also to wait and, therefore, that the elections must be postponed for a year, ostensibly to give time for a revision of the franchise.

The final agreement provided for the accession of Aden to the Federation on March 1, 1963, and was subject to the approval of the British parliament and the legislatures of the Federation and Aden. It provided that Aden would become a state, that is, it would no longer be a colony, when it joined the Federation. The new constitution for Aden would provide for national government with a Legislative Council of twenty-three members, of whom sixteen would be elected (instead of twelve), the remainder being nominated by the High Commissioner except for the ex-officio Attorney General.

The judicial system of Aden would remain intact with additional safeguards against interference from the federal government and the right of citizens of Aden to appeal to the Court of Appeal in East Africa or the Privy Council in London would remain. A Federal High Court would be established to act as a court of first instance on disputes concerning the constitution, or between the federal government and individual states, or between individual states themselves, or in cases where federal officers neglected their duties or exceeded their rights; it would act as a court of appeal for any state asking for an interpretation of constitutional provisions and would advise the Federal Supreme Council on interpretation of the constitution. The judges of the Federal High Court would be given security of office and any appeals from its decisions would be referred to the Judicial Committee of the Privy Council.

The agreement provided for the division of responsibilities between the federal and state governments, the control and safeguards of the civil service and the financial organisation of the Federation as prepared by Mr Pearl. There were special safeguards which had been included specifically to satisfy Aden: the constitution could be reviewed after three years but the Federal Council could not change it except with a two-thirds majority of the total members of the Council, and even then any three states could object to the law being passed, in which case it had to go back to the Federal Council and secure a four-fifths vote. If any state objected, the Federal Council could not consider any alteration in the representation of any state or the list of federal and state subjects—thus Aden alone would have the right of veto. Finally, after a trial period of six years, Aden could call for a conference to discuss its case if it felt itself unfairly treated. The conference would have a British minister as chairman, and if Britain considered the Aden case to be just, could ask the Federation to rectify the matter and, if this were refused, could withdraw Aden from the Federation.*

There was also to be a Code of Fundamental Human Rights. This had been drafted and, when approved by the British parliament and the two Councils, it would be issued by Britain as an Order in Council. No federal law could interfere with the Code. This again was primarily of concern to Aden which enjoyed rights not existing in the tribal areas and unlikely to be applied there.†

The British right to withdraw Aden from the Federation was contained in a draft treaty between the British government and the Federation, which accompanied the agreement. The treaty also gave Britain the right to exclude or withdraw from the Federation any area or areas *within* Aden, if this was considered necessary for its world-wide defences. The object of this provision was to make it possible for Britain to establish a sovereign base area of the type existing in Cyprus.

Britain agreed to pay the Colony £500,000 over the first three years to meet the burden of costs associated with the merger, and to pay £200,000 a year to the federal government to compensate for customs revenues which it would refund to individual states when the customs union was established.

The degree of doubt about union still existing in Aden was clear from the campaign launched by the ministers over the broadcasting station as soon as they got home. The powerful Trades Union Congress had formed a political party, the Peoples Socialist Party, just before the London conference. Its leader was the highly

---

*It was calculated that the six-year period would carry Aden through two elections. As Sir Charles Johnston explains (op. cit., p. 112) it was feared that a wave of anti-federal emotion, after the first elections and before the working of the system was established, could lead to unjustifiable demands for revision.

†'The Federal Ministers watched the process with cynical tolerance' while the Code was being discussed in London in July; Johnston, op. cit., p. 116.

intelligent Abdullah al-Asnaj, a man of great organising ability and eloquence who could almost certainly count more heads in his support than any other leader. Its opposition was inevitable, for it rejected the Federation on the grounds that it did not include Yemen, and the constitutional changes on the grounds that a new constitution should be framed only after elections held under a new franchise that included the Yemeni population. The TUC had given a taste of things to come by calling a twenty-four-hour general strike on July 23, 1962, to protest against the London conference. The Luqman group, to which Abdullah Saidi had belonged, was also against the merger taking place before elections, and some important business men were opposed to it altogether. There was therefore a wide spectrum of opposition. Bayoomi's United National Party provided the only organised support but there was a substantial section of unorganised conservative opinion behind the government, and many of the influential religious leaders supported federation with the Protectorate states because it would mean a Shafei union and exclude the heretical Zeidis of Yemen.

The opponents objected primarily to the minority nature of the government which had been formed in 1959 on a 27 per cent vote of an electorate totalling 21,500 out of a population of 180,000. To this Bayoomi replied on September 2 that the fact that many electors 'misguidedly' boycotted the election did not alter the fact that the government was properly elected or alter its responsibilities to the electorate. To the question as to why the franchise had not been revised earlier to enable elections to be held before the decision was reached, he answered: 'The franchise is one of the most complicated questions in local policies. The Aden Government therefore thought it proper to wait for revision of the franchise until this could be done by the national government of a new State of Aden which should come into existence at the next stage of Aden's constitutional advance.' V. K. Joshi, the only Indian member of the government, had broadcast in similar terms on August 24, adding: 'There is good reason to believe that one of the first acts of the national government will be to consider and introduce new electoral qualifications before the holding of fresh elections. Amendment of the franchise is bound to take some time. Qualifications for the franchise will require to be settled, the necessary legislation to be made and the electoral roll to be revised in the light of the new franchise.' Bayoomi also replied, on August 21, to the complaint that no date had been fixed for independence by saying that, although independence was inevitable, to fix a date at that stage would make this serious question 'an issue for cheap and electioneering propaganda; various parties would naturally try to claim that they could get independence for this country in less time, without considering whether the basic essentials of a State are first achieved or not. . . . We want a fully matured independence.'*

There was, in fact, a clear indication that complete independence was a long way off in the provision for Britain to withdraw Aden from the Federation, if necessary, after six years. Almost all the safeguards provided for the Adenis against the federal government were based on the right of Britain to intervene, on their right to appeal to the highest British judicial authorities, or on the High Commissioner's right to intervene in such matters as the rights of the civil servants. Another minister, Abdullah Basendwah, argued on August 22 that federation was 'a necessary step on the road to independence'; but, in fact, it was the lack of independence that alone made federation possible at that time.

There were other objections to the British connection, over the continued existence of the British base and slowness in the Adenisation programme. On the first point, the ministers replied quite simply that Aden had no means of defending itself without British forces, that the £11 million spent by them every year was one cause of Aden's booming prosperity, and the base was the largest employer of labour in the Colony. Bayoomi, broadcasting on September 14 about Adenisation, said the problem was to keep the British civil servants because there were not enough local officers of adequate training and experience to staff government departments completely and 'it would take time to overcome the difficulty . . .'. Mohammed Husseini, the Minister of Education, making the same point five

*These broadcasts were published by the Aden government in an undated pamphlet called *Questions and Answers*.

days earlier, had stressed that Adenisation should proceed as rapidly as possible, adding that the ministers of the Federation and Aden had recommended that their governments should formulate a common policy regarding 'Arabisation' of the public service 'on the basis of definitions to be established by a joint committee'.

Such was the need to convince the existing civil servants and those students who desired to join that Husseini again spoke at greater length on the subject on the same day as Bayoomi. He pointed out that, since the inception of the policy in 1959, the government had given the highest priority to training people at home and overseas. 'Every single Adenese candidate with the necessary minimum qualifications is sent at public expense for training overseas with a view to fitting him in due course for a high post in government service', he said; and he listed the domestic training courses: a two-year course for clerks, a teacher training college for men and another for women giving two-year courses for 100 teachers, a police training school for 100 trainees a year, a training school for 60 nurses a year, and the internal training schemes of the government departments themselves. But, he stressed, there were insufficient candidates with the necessary quality for training.

Other broadcasts stressed that labour would not become a federal subject and that therefore the rights and privileges of the trades unions would continue to be the responsibility of the Aden government and state legislature and that all the courts would operate as before. There would be, said W. G. Bryce, the Attorney General, on September 8, 'the same insistence on the rules designed to guard against injustice as before; and there are guarantees for this—it is not just a case of saying so'. Internal security would remain the responsibility of the High Commissioner in Aden and not be a federal matter.

Mohammed Husseini said on August 31 that it was laid down that the federal Minister of Education should do nothing to impair the educational system in Aden and should pay special attention to the provision of seven years of primary and intermediate education for every child born in Aden, to providing night-school post-intermediate training for children who did not qualify for secondary schools, and to giving financial assistance to help meritorious children to continue their studies overseas. Basendwah, the Minister of Health and Immigration, similarly stressed that the Aden health service would not suffer and that progress would be maintained. He then listed an extensive development plan for the health services which he insisted, would continue unimpeded by federation; and he pointed out that it was in the interest of the federal states, whose people used the Aden health service, to see that its improvement continued.

Great attention was paid to the fact that, with British help, the Colony would not lose by the formation of the customs union*, and the economic condition and future of Aden was discussed at great length. Bayoomi warned on September 14 that if Aden did not join, the Federation would probably build its own port and might regulate the flow across the frontier of the labour on which Aden largely depended. Aden was vulnerable geographically, politically and economically; the frontiers were just 'a line on the map'. 'The economic survival of Aden is dependent on accession', Bayoomi declared. More cheerfully, Ali al-Saffi stated, on August 27, that the removal of customs barriers and road improvements would greatly help trade. Aden merchants, he said, had already seen an increase of trade in the three years since the Federation was formed; in 1961, the Aden Wholesale Co-operative Market had handled £5 million worth of imported fresh fruit and vegetables. He continued:

Aden's prosperity has hitherto been based on the entrepôt trade —for example the buying of skins from Ethiopia and the sale of the same skins to America, and the buying of coffee from Ethiopia and its sale to Europe. The first of these trades has been reduced by 35 per cent in the last seven years and the second has declined by about 65 per cent in the same period. To counterbalance this loss in the entrepôt trade, however, there has been a 50 per cent increase of the trade within Aden itself, largely due to the increased population and the British forces living there. But there

---

*'Aden . . . will be joining a large customs union at no cost to itself'; Husseini, August 20. 'In other words, money paid by Aden residents will not go to finance projects outside the State of Aden'; Ali al-Saffi, August 27.

is every possibility that the entrepôt trade will continue to decline and it is by looking to the interior that Aden can keep its prosperity. With the removal of customs duty the way to this market is wide open.

The primary importance of the British base and the port was stressed. Basendwah pointed out on August 22 that the port was the key to the future and it was essential that the atmosphere of internal confidence and goodwill should be preserved in order to continue to attract world shipping. Al-Saffi stressed the damage being done by labour troubles.

Speaking of the base, Husseini said on August 22 that it would be a bad thing if Aden should be dependent on British money for ever, and pointed out that this was precisely the reason why the Governor had stated in his January address to the Legislative Council that Aden should broaden the base of its economy 'so that it should not suffer from a bad trade depression when the British base leaves Aden'. Aden and the Federation could not live in watertight compartments; the economy should be developed in the context of the whole area. 'Aden's merger with the Federation', he continued, 'will provide scope for far wider economic development and, with the continued assistance of the wealth provided by the British base, will bring us more quickly to the time when Aden, as part of the Federation, will be proud of its own wealth and proud of its own ability to sustain its own economic independence.'

Al-Saffi reaffirmed on September 9 that development would continue. 'As a result of the visit of representatives of the Commonwealth Development Organisation in October 1961 plans have been made for the development of Aden and the Protectorate as a whole.' The British government had already agreed to improve roads and schemes for agriculture and irrigation were already in mind. 'These developments do not necessarily depend on Aden's accession to the Federation', he said, 'but they will be much facilitated by it.'

It was difficult to judge to what extent this mixture of good sense and special pleading affected public opinion, or to assess whether it made headway against the inflammatory incitement from Cairo radio. It possibly convinced some of the better educated indigenous Adenese who had, on balance, a higher standard of living and more opportunities than the non-resident, disenfranchised labourers who constituted a majority of the population and were mostly Yemenis. Perhaps no sense or eloquence could have made headway against their bitterness as second-class citizens. And this was the tinder of trouble.

II

Neither the Governor nor the Aden government was prepared to take any chances in the five weeks between the return of the Ministers from London and the scheduled meeting of the Legislative Council on September 24, 1962, when the merger plan came up for approval. Sir Charles Johnston considered that the merger was a matter of life and death to the half-a-million inhabitants of the federal area, and held that it would have been 'a strange misapplication of our [British] principles' to allow the Adenese to prevent it, thus severing the Federation from the sea and driving them towards Yemen.* In other words, the merger would not be stopped by opposition in Aden.

The Governor decided to give the People's Socialist Party (PSP) of Abdullah al-Asnaj the right to speak once in each quarter of Aden during the five weeks' period. Bayoomi's party was given similar permission. This was not equality of treatment, since the ministers were broadcasting about federation almost daily. On the other hand, the opposition had the full support of Cairo and Sanaa radio stations. Processions were banned altogether because they were more likely to develop into riots, but Asnaj defied this order by calling on the people of Aden to march on the Legislative Council on September 24.

Meanwhile he held his authorised meetings until September 15, when he and two of his associates were sentenced to a fortnight in gaol for marching in procession to the mosque of blind Sheikh Beihani, a supporter of federation. This neatly arranged for his absence from the scene at the time of the vote. Yet it equally suited Asnaj to have no part in the bigger troubles to come, for which he

*Johnston, op. cit., p. 195.

would otherwise certainly be blamed, and his absence at this moment would enable him to renew agitation after the vote. To convince the Aden public that the government would have no nonsense, security exercises were held several times in the last fortnight and the licence of the pro-PSP newspaper was suspended.

These actions did not prevent riots on the morning of September 24, when crowds began to assemble not long after dawn. The general strike called by the TUC was a complete success. The idle throng quickly swelled the first organised assemblies in Crater and began to march by several routes through the town to the Legislative Council building, a former church perched high on a hill and therefore very easily defended by the police. Tempers quickly mounted when an Arab officer caught in the mob wounded two men with his revolver. Demonstrators reached a point almost at the foot of the hill but never got beyond it, and, as the Council debate proceeded acrimoniously inside the building, the rioting went on at various points in Crater. The police used tear gas and fired some shots but the damage was much less than might have been expected, largely because the police used restraint and applied a well-prepared plan which prevented separate mobs from coalescing below the hill, and also because the mobs were not out to destroy their own property. Nevertheless, the disorders were so widespread in Aden late in the morning that the authorities deployed three platoons of British troops to reinforce the hard-pressed police. The rioters pulled up watermains and flooded one area of Crater, destroyed cars outside the headquarters of Bayoomi's United National Party, and burnt the newspaper office of *Al-Kifah*, a newspaper owned by Bayoomi's brother, which had strongly supported the federal proposals. The total casualties for the day were five wounded and one dead.*

The debate lasted two and a half days, but for the last day and a half there were no more disorders although the atmosphere was

---

*The official story was that only 3,000 Yemenis took part. How one recognises Yemenis in a seething mob of Adenis I do not know and how one counts a mob has always baffled me, but it was the impression of my colleagues and me that over Crater as a whole the number was much greater and that Adenis were involved.

uneasily poised on the edge of trouble all the time. An opposition amendment contesting Bayoomi's motion in support of the London Agreement was defeated by sixteen votes to seven, with two of the Adeni nominated members voting with five of the elected members against the proposal. The seven opponents then walked out of the Chamber and were followed by another member who said he did so because he had been insulted during the debate. The London Agreement was then approved by the remaining fifteen voting members. It was a victory that gave little cause for satisfaction, for the fifteen included five British ex-officio members, two European-nominated members and the five ministers who had made the agreement, which meant that only three of the remaining eleven members of the Council had been converted to approval of the plan. (The Federal Council went through the formality of approving the agreement next day.)

The most significant fact was that the seven opposition members who withdrew represented small, moderate bourgeois political groups, and they and the People's Socialist Party covered the greater part of active political opinion in Aden. It meant that on this issue a large part of moderate opinion had sided with their erstwhile enemies, the PSP, and left the small party of Hassan Ali Bayoomi and the other four ministers in uncomfortable political isolation. It furthermore left them vulnerable to threats from extremists which eventually some had not the courage to ignore. They had all been subject to some villainous forms of intimidation before the debate, and the bold Bayoomi, the only one whose strength and cunning equalled that of Abdullah al-Asnaj, already possessed a dossier of menaces.

It was said officially that some of those who voted against the plan did so because they were intimidated, but it is doubtful whether more than one was influenced in this way. The most powerful attacks on the plan in the Council were made by Ali Mohammed Luqman (son of Mohammed Ali), a poet and journalist, and the former minister, Abdullah Saidi. The range of their criticism covered all the objections of the Adenis that the ministers had tried to counter in their broadcasts, but the core of their argument was that the choice was not that of Aden but of Britain. 'It is Hobson's choice', declared Luqman, a neat reference to the Governor's Adviser in Aden, Laurence Hobson, who had been and still was the outrider for the Governor in ministerial circles and the *suq* of Crater.

The failure to secure the support of these people of moderate opinion, which did serious harm to the evolution of the plan, could possibly have been avoided. Everyone agreed in principle with the policy of Federation and the moderates did not demand the removal of the British base.* They were not anti-British. Although they demanded free elections under a new franchise before Aden agreed to join the Federation, they did not, in fact, expect this to happen, and it is almost certain that a greater degree of consultation could have reduced their opposition to public dissent and secured their tacit acceptance, which would have been expressed possibly in abstention rather than a counter-vote. Luqman and some of his friends said they had had no contact with the Governor for several months until they attended a reception on the eve of the departure for the London conference, and that they then had the impression, rightly or wrongly, that no final decision on the plan would be taken in London and before private consultations.† The failure to keep these moderates on the side-line deprived the government of useful men who could muster group support. When at last they called on Abdel Qawee Mackawee, a trusted, if not brilliant, publicity director of the big Besse firm, he came to power under the shadow of death at the hands of extremists and soon went over to the other side.

On the day after the Legislative Council's vote there was a dramatic change in the context of the Aden situation. The Imam's family was overthrown and a republic declared in Yemen.

---

*Even the PSP was not as rigid as it seemed on the surface. Abdullah al-Asnaj told the author that the party stood for union with Yemen and the removal of the British base, although union would have tied Aden to a country where trades unions were not allowed to exist and the removal of the base would have put most of the party's members out of work. He added, however, that an 'independent Aden Government might feel justified in revising these policies'.

†To the author, on the night of the vote.

III

The three years that had elapsed since the formation of the Federation of the Amirates of South Arabia were remarkably quiet on the Yemen frontier, but this was due more to the internal situation in Yemen than to the vigorous counter-action of the British in 1958. The conflict of aims between the Imam and ex-Sultan Ali of Lahej had also helped to keep down trouble by preventing combined action.

Early in 1959, there was serious famine in Yemen and the Imam agreed to accept 15,000 tons of wheat from the United States which he had refused in the preceding autumn. Ahmed's suspicion of his communist helpers continued to grow despite Badr's influence.*

As previously noted, he accepted the United States Ambassador to Cairo as Minister to Yemen, and was offered American technical and financial aid to build a road from Taiz to Sanaa to link-up with the Hodeida-Sanaa road, then being built by communist Chinese. It was a sign of the changed atmosphere that Sir William Luce and his wife paid a visit to the British Chargé d'Affaires in Taiz in November.

The first serious signs of trouble inside Yemen occurred in January 1960, when Taiz was put under military control after the discovery of pamphlets against the Imam signed by the 'Free Yemeni Officers'. When the Imam went to Rome in April to cure his morphine addiction, contracted when taking treatment for arthritis, Prince Mohammed al-Badr had further trouble in Taiz with army officers and high officials, and the trouble spread to Hodeida and Sanaa. Badr bribed the powerful group of Hashid tribes in the north to stand by him, promised the army more pay, and then arrested some top officials and executed some of his other opponents.

The Imam did not get back to Yemen until August and was extremely suspicious of Badr's dealings with the Hashid which had all the symptoms of a typical family plot to secure power. There

---

*A correspondent of *The Economist* reported on July 25, 1959 that there were 200 European communists established in all government departments and that 700 Chinese were working in the country.

were more reasons than this to be suspicious. The behaviour of Prince Mohammed after his father's departure suggested that he believed the old man's health was irreparable, and that by leaving Yemen, which was forbidden to the Imam by tradition, he had lost a great deal of his support. The old man had hardly been gone a month when his Regent purged many of his men in the administration and the army and established a representative council of seven members in Sanaa as a token of the changing pattern of government. This was in keeping with Badr's image as a supporter of President Nasser and with his reputation for wanting to modernise the medieval administration of the country. Radio Sanaa paid fulsome tributes to him: 'Yemen abounds with hope, particularly since the people realise the genius of the Crown Prince, who traces the outline of the enlightened future with far-sighted wisdom.'

Badr's campaign was handicapped by the fact that the Yemenis had both a wholesome fear of Ahmed and also a deal of contempt for him, so that, when the Imam got off the boat at Hodeida and made a bloodthirsty speech with all the healthy vigour of former days, many of the people who had thrown in their lot with Badr hit the trail for Aden as fast as they could. The Imam refused to talk to Badr, cancelled the bribe to the Hashid, and sent troops with artillery and armoured vehicles to the north in December to suppress the consequent trouble. He also closed down the air force and police training schools which Badr had established and which were run by Egyptian officers, and expelled Yahya Harsi, the former commander of the Lahej forces who had defected to Yemen and whose sixteen-year-old daughter Badr had married. The reconciliation of the prince with his father did not take place until October.

On his way back from Rome, the Imam had a meeting with President Nasser in Cairo which did nothing to improve their relations, as Imam Ahmed's subsequent actions demonstrated. Early in 1960, Prince Mohammed asked Nasser for 1,000 soldiers but Nasser replied directly to his father to the effect that he could have troops to defend himself against an external enemy but not to suppress his own people. The Imam thereupon recalled his representative from Cairo, which virtually ended the Yemeni connection with the United Arab Republic. (Nasser's contempt for the arrangement with Yemen was evident by the fact that he forgot to terminate it formally until December 25, 1961 'because of the reactionary and repressive nature of the regime'.) The Imam also sent a representative to the anniversary celebrations of the revolution in Iraq, with which country Nasser was on bad terms at the time.

Nasser now worked openly against the Imam. In December 1961, tribal leaders from the southern regions of Yemen and the Protectorate frontiers, all of them opponents of their respective governments, assembled in Cairo and had several meetings with the National Union of Egypt—Egypt's only popular organisation—in an effort to secure arms and money for rebellion. Radio Cairo continued its campaign against alleged repression in the Protectorates without reference to Yemen's claim and, indeed, spoke always of 'the Arab South', not of South Yemen. The visit of the tribesmen was understood to mean that Nasser was now supporting the Free Yemeni movement against the Imam and was seeking to renew frontier troubles which the Imam had almost completely halted for over a year.

Although both Imam Ahmed and Prince Mohammed al-Badr had attacked the formation of the Federation of the Amirates of the South neither had done much about it, and under the soothing influence of Sir William Luce in Aden the situation was unusually calm. Just before he departed for Rome, the Imam had sent a delegation to Aden to discuss frontier problems, but these had come to nothing because his representatives would not talk to the federal ministers and were doing some quiet subversion on the side. There was still a fair amount of gun-running over the frontier, and in March 1961, the Aden government mounted a major military operation called 'Canister' to stop it. (This gun-running may have been the result of the tribal leaders' visit to Cairo, for the captured arms were of Czech origin from Egypt.) Sir William Luce paid a courtesy visit to Badr in Taiz in June to see what impression he could make on his Egyptian sympathies.* There was a frontier incident at Rahida in August, but otherwise the frontiers remained quiet in 1960.

*He travelled in a Russian helicopter which crashed at Taiz airport, fortunately without killing anyone.

Whether from the momentum of Badr's liberalism of 1959, or by conspiracy conceived in the tribal leaders' visit to Cairo or by natural resurgence of popular feeling against an ageing Imam, disturbances occurred in Yemen again in the middle of 1960. There were bomb incidents in June, and, when several people were killed by bombs in Taiz and Ibb in July, the Imam imposed a curfew in all central and southern towns in Yemen. This created a brief period of calm, but in November there were more bomb outrages and the police in that month seized dynamite in a convoy. The trouble was very close to the seat of power, for the private secretary of the Imam and twenty other senior officials were arrested. The tide was running strongly against the Imam, for the pardon he offered to refugees did not induce any to return and there was a continuing flow of dissident tribesmen back to the Protectorates. The Free Yemeni movement was active in Aden again, and when the Imam discovered that explosives were being sent from the Colony he upbraided the British Chargé d'Affaires on December 30 and threatened to break off diplomatic relations.

In March 1961, there was an attempt on the Imam's life as he was opening a new hospital at Hodeida. He received four wounds, four of his bodyguard were killed and several others wounded. He was then sixty-eight and in poor health, but Badr, who was abroad, flew back from Rome with medical specialists and Ahmed survived. His health nevertheless was further damaged and the tribal chiefs who were on his side, and other supporters, insisted that he should designate his successor. This he did in October 1961, in a broadcast to the people from Sanaa calling on them to give their support to Prince Mohammed al-Badr whom he described as 'their future representative'. He could not be more precise than this since the office of Imam was elective. Nevertheless unrest continued in the country. It was said that the dissidence now came, not from a demand for the earlier policies of Badr, but for the policy associated with Prince Hassan, the brother of Ahmed, a man of more liberal temperament who had been Ahmed's rival at the time of the assassination of their father Yahya and who had lived outside Yemen almost ever since.

On September 9, 1962, Imam Ahmed died and Prince Mohammed succeeded him. Badr was a weak and foolish man who had sought to establish his position in Yemen by enlisting the support of President Nasser and by basking in the sunshine of the Egyptian leader's reputation: a policy that made sure he would lose the support of traditional tribal leaders without gaining the support of the radicals who hated the Muttawakkilite family. Only eighteen days after the old Imam's death, one of these radicals, Colonel Abdullah al-Sallal who had been a prisoner of Ahmed for several years, chained to the wall of a cave, and had been released by the intervention of Badr, expressed his gratitude by leading the army with six tanks against Al-Bashayan Palace in Taiz and shelling it. The palace guard fought back until overpowered and Sallal occupied the damaged building, whereupon he announced that Badr was dead and buried in the débris. In time-honoured Yemeni fashion—which Prince Abdullah had fatally failed to follow in 1955—Sallal executed those members of the royal family and its friends whom he could lay his hands on. He then proclaimed himself leader of the revolution with the title of Prime Minister.

Small contingents of Egyptian troops arrived to support the revolution. It was welcomed virtually everywhere in the Arab world except by the governments of Saudi Arabia and Jordan. On October 8, Sallal received a party of foreign correspondents, who subsequently reported that all was under control. Sanaa radio described the tribes as 'flocking to submit'. But, on October 15, the Arab League received a message purporting to come from Imam Mohammed al-Badr and there were rumours that Prince Hassan, his uncle, who had been at the United Nations when the coup took place, was organising resistance in the mountains of Yemen. It was beyond doubt before the month ended that there was fighting between the republicans and the royalists at Saada and Harad in the north and at Harib and Marib in the east. Then, on November 9, Badr reappeared in Saudi Arabia to meet pressmen and explain that he had escaped over the wall of his palace and, with five of his bodyguard, had made his way across country to the Saudi frontier, gathering tribal support on his way.

IV

The revolution in Yemen had a profound effect on the situation in Aden and the Federation. The weakness of the policy of the People's Socialist Party and other extreme radical elements was that the rule of Imam Ahmed was the most repressive and reactionary in the Arab world, so that, while they called for democratic rights in Aden, they were at the same time calling for union with a country where no civil rights were granted. A substantial part of the Yemeni population of Aden itself consisted of people who had for many years supported the Free Yemeni movement against the Imamate, and these would have been the last to submit themselves again to its rule. It seemed that all was now changed. Yemen had put itself in the vanguard of the Arab national movement and had the support of the supreme leader, Nasser, and almost everyone in the Arab world. Opposition to the Aden government, the British and the federal plan was strengthened as a result.

The Governor and government of Aden were in no doubt that the developments in Yemen should not be allowed to interfere with the well-laid plans to unite Aden with the Federation, but there were grounds for anxiety in the debate on British policy taking place in London. The revolution in Yemen touched the very core of the problem of policy in the Middle East: should Britain make sufficient concessions to President Nasser and radical Arab nationalism everywhere in order to secure mutual tolerance? Or should its policy be based on the defence of existing interests and fulfilment of existing commitments, even though this meant opposition to Nasser and his movement? The choice would be expressed in Yemen in the recognition or non-recognition of the republican government, although in theory the decision was supposed to depend on the ability of that government to control or not control the territory. (In mid-autumn 1962, the republicans, with about 10,000 Egyptian troops, were in control of about two-thirds of the country, including the central triangle contained by Sanaa, Taiz and Hodeida.)

There were powerful voices in London contending that British interests could be best served by recognition, which would coincide with the mass of effective Arab opinion, remove the stigma that Britain was always on the side of reactionary rulers, and do something to improve the evil reputation the British had had ever since the Suez invasion. It was argued that, by coming to terms over Yemen and thereby securing a large measure of popular support in South Arabia and elsewhere in the Middle East, the British would have a better chance of making arrangements that would preserve the military base for as long as they wanted to keep it. The alternative, it was contended, was to damage the British position further in the main Arab countries and face military problems in South Arabia, which would be much greater than any experienced before by reason of the military potential the Egyptians could provide from Yemen to support the already enlarged popular resistance movement.* As the debate went on through the latter part of 1962, events seem to support this thesis. In December, the United States government recognised the republican regime, with the face-saving (but useless) proviso, included for the benefit of Saudi Arabia, that Egypt would reduce its military commitments in Yemen. On December 28, Egyptian rockets were displayed at a military parade in Sanaa, and the British base began to take precautions against their use.† Sallal had meanwhile broadcast an announcement of the formation of the Republic of the Arab Peninsula, an ambitious fancy implying impending revolt in Saudi Arabia, South Arabia and the Persian Gulf states and sheikhdoms.

The thesis was steadfastly resisted by the authorities in Aden and by the federal rulers, who saw at once the danger to their joint plan and to the rulers personally. The plan had only just scraped through the Aden legislature; as Sir Charles Johnston himself pointed out later, a day's delay would have brought the vote *after* the Yemen revolution and so could have led to the rejection of the merger.‡ If the British government did not stand fast against the militant extremists in Aden and the claims of Cairo and Yemen,

*This issue split the Foreign Office, as it did the Conservative and Labour parties.
†The precautions were reported by the Defence Correspondent of *The Times*.
‡Johnston, op. cit.

the ground gained since 1959, and much more into the bargain, would be lost. Far from the military base being more secure, it would lose the support of friends whose moderation made agreement about it possible and be surrounded by enemies who could never be sure of their own success until they got rid of it. The Aden authorities and the rulers therefore opposed recognition of the Yemeni republican government, and called for a strong hand in dealing with troubles inside Aden itself.

A party of federal ministers went to London early in October 1962 to press their case both for the merger and for more firmness. They were fortunate in having Duncan Sandys as Minister of State for the Colonies, since he had not the slightest intention of conciliating Nasser or those whom he regarded as plain mischief-makers in Aden, and was ready to fight the Foreign Office or any members of the cabinet guilty of what he considered woolly thinking in regard to a deal with left-wing Arab nationalism. As the government was united and firm in its decision to keep the Aden base, he was in due course able to convince his colleagues that it was much better to hold the area, by force if necessary—and there was adequate force available—than to gamble on either the good faith or good sense of Britain's opponents in the region.

Although the federal ministers were convinced of Sandys' intentions, they were not too happy about the state of British opinion at the time of their visit, and they departed with a lurking fear that they might still be let down. The situation was at its worst in early October because there was no evidence of any royalist resistance to the republic, and it therefore seemed inevitable that the republic would be recognised by Britain. In Aden the populace was solidly on the side of the republic, and all over the Crater bazaar area its flag was being flown from shops and houses. Free Yemenis were streaming across the frontier, bound to their brave new world, taking with them all they could carry in furniture, fittings and trade goods to begin again their commercial life at home.

Even in the tribal areas the message was having its effect on simple people whose ears were glued to their transistor radios. Those who had been educated, including young officers in the security forces, were thinking new thoughts and beginning to dream new dreams that boded ill for the old ways of life. Mohammed Husseini, the Minister for Posts, Telephones and Electricity, who had been hand-picked to replace Ali Salem Ali when he resigned early in the merger talks, resigned when visiting London to discuss plans for television in Aden, stating that 'to dissociate or separate any of the people of the South is practically impossible'. Two other Aden ministers were wavering.*

Bayoomi never wavered in face of popular opinion or the hesitations of the British government, calculating that the security of the base would be the decisive factor in the end. When it became known that there was royalist resistance and that Imam Mohammed al-Badr was alive and speaking, the situation somewhat improved, at least as far as the British government was concerned, for it was now much easier to argue against recognition. Although the debate went on for a long time afterwards behind the scenes, the government decided against it and in favour of standing by its existing policy in South Arabia. On November 13, 1962, the House of Commons passed the merger Bill.

This meant the strong hand in Aden. The Secretary of State had already sent out Nigel Morris, a former Commissioner of Police in Singapore and later Deputy Inspector-General of Colonial Police, to take charge of security in Aden while the Colony rode what the authorities believed would be only a temporary storm. The Governor appointed Bayoomi, who had been complaining about the namby-pamby methods used against the extremists, as Ministerial Adviser on Security, in order to contribute local knowledge to Morris's expertise. The Aden authorities acted promptly when Yemeni and Protectorate leaders of the Port Labour Union called a strike (which was illegal under the 1960 Labour Ordinance), by deporting them from the Colony. Then, when the PSP issued a pamphlet about the anti-Federation riots of September 24, they made this the pretext for arresting Asnaj and two of his associates,

*Husseini did not resign until November 16, after the House of Commons had passed the merger Bill, but by early October he had turned against the merger, and he advised against it while in London.

once again on charges of sedition, for which Asnaj was sentenced to a year's imprisonment. The sentence was eventually quashed by the East African Court of Appeal after Aden had joined the Federation and Asnaj had been released under a general amnesty, but it had served its purpose: he had been successfully kept out of the way during the critical winter months.

The policy of firmness had its effect. The arrests and expulsions weakened the Aden TUC, and its strike called for November 19 was only partially successful. Firmness also reassured the Protectorate leaders, who received Duncan Sandys with cordiality when he arrived early in December for a brief visit. The British were, in fact, taking no action to prevent the passage of arms through the Protectorate area to the royalists, and the Governor's aide de camp was giving clandestine help to them. Although he was said to be doing this without the knowledge of the Governor, no one believed this, least of all the federal rulers, who concluded that the British were now wholly behind the royalists.

With the situation apparently well in hand, it was decided to press forward as fast as possible with the merger. As a first step, the Governor and Bayoomi summoned the Aden Legislative Council to elect the four councillors needed to replace the four British ex-officio members, who were due to retire under the constitutional changes. This should have been done much earlier, but the conditions hitherto had been so adverse that it would have been difficult to find candidates; in the changed circumstances no less than fifty-one offered themselves. As the opposition group in the Council boycotted the elections, candidates all favourable to the merger were, in effect, chosen by Bayoomi. On January 7, 1963, the president of the Aden TUC was sent to prison for four months for calling the strike on November 19. Nine days later, on January 16, the chairman of the Federal Supreme Council signed the draft treaty between Britain and the Federation. The Orders in Council for Aden's entry into the Federation were issued in London on January 17. Next day Aden was in the Federation, the amendments of the Federal Constitution became effective, the constitutional changes in Aden were introduced, and the Governor became the High Commissioner for

Aden and the Protectorate of South Arabia. The Federation of the Amirates of the South, no longer a correct designation, became the Federation of South Arabia.

Bayoomi, as Chief Minister of Aden, became Minister without Portfolio in the federal government and took with him as Minister of Education his deputy in the United National Party, Abdul Rahman Girgerah, a newspaper proprietor and editor. Sayid Omar Shihab, Minister of Finance, and Abu Bakr Koadel, Minister of Posts and Telegraphs, were the other two Adenis appointed to the federal cabinet, but neither they nor Girgerah had had ministerial experience. The Aden government was completely changed, with the exception of Bayoomi, so that no one could say that those who had worked for the merger had benefited by it.

5

The Start of the Struggle

HASSAN ALI BAYOOMI'S flesh succumbed before his spirit. More than any other Adeni, he had borne the brunt of the battle for federation, although he was diabetic and not half as strong as his external appearance suggested. In addition to the many anxieties imposed on him by the long period of negotiations, he had braved unpopularity with the public and the constant threat of death at the hands of the extremists; but, unlike many of his colleagues, he stayed unshaken by it all. As Minister of Labour he had carried through the 1960 Industrial Ordinance, which Sir William Luce formulated on expert advice to curb the wave of strikes then damaging the trade of the port, and the workers had never forgiven him for it. This made it difficult for him to bridge the gap between himself and the unions when he became Chief Minister; and there were many other more moderate groups who resented his high-handed conduct of affairs.

As soon as he became Chief Minister, he tried to conciliate opinion. At the same time he asserted his new rights with the British authorities in Aden who found difficulty at first in adjusting themselves to the greater degree of domestic authority the Aden government acquired by the constitutional change. He was not beset by these troubles long, however. In April 1963, he had a heart attack; though he recovered from it enough to go to London by ship for further treatment, he died there in June. No one can now know to what extent his skill and strength in handling his own people, the federal rulers and the British, would have affected events, but he was undoubtedly a man in the mould of Nuri al-Said and might have managed things as astutely in Aden as Nuri did in Iraq for so many years. Like Nuri, too, and for that matter Gamal Abdel Nasser, Bayoomi came of modest family and had risen to leadership by his own efforts.

He was replaced by Sayyid Zein Baharoon, one of his own men and a successful merchant of good family in Aden. Aged only thirty-two, he was newly come to political life when the Legislative Council elected four members to replace the British in December 1962. Bayoomi had appointed him Minister of Finance. Baharoon reformed the cabinet, bringing back Ali Salem Ali as Minister of Labour, a post from which it was hoped he might put his friendly contacts with the trades unions to some advantage, and made Abdullah Basendwah Minister of Finance. The administration was less one-sided than that of Bayoomi.

I

The merger and the Aden government were two lonely and un-wanted children. The merchant and conservative elements who had favoured their birth regarded them with as much doubt as hope, and the larger mass of opposition opinion was not changed by the more moderate complexion of Baharoon's cabinet. Nevertheless, for a few months after the merger, the situation was relatively calm, despite the propaganda of the PSP, and the broadcasts of Cairo and Sanaa. Abdullah al-Asnaj emerged from prison only to depart shortly afterwards for Cairo to devise plans for the future. The strong tide of national opinion after the revolution in Yemen had ebbed a little as the military situation there gave promise of a long drawn-out struggle.

The Federal Supreme Council proposed in May 1963 that the goal should be independence in 1969 and that the British should then take out a lease for the military base. Kennedy Trevaskis, the High Commissioner-designate, took the proposal to London. In October, Peter Thornycroft, the Minister of Defence, spent three days in Aden discussing this matter and the general security situation with the ministers of Aden and the Federation, and a month later Trevaskis, now High Commissioner, went back to London for consultations.*

The problem of the elections, which had been postponed in Aden from January 1963 to January 1964, loomed large because the question of the franchise had to be settled first. Baharoon was successful in getting together a seven-man committee of all political parties to draft a new franchise; but when Trevaskis took the committee report with him to London in November, Duncan Sandys rejected it because he considered that it discriminated too sharply against Commonwealth citizens and would have excluded many, mainly Indians, from the electoral roll. This compelled Baharoon to postpone the elections for another six months.

The situation was not made any easier by the activities of the United Nations, where the Special Committee on Colonialism decided in May 1963 to send a committee to investigate the Aden problem, although the British Delegate, Sir Patrick Dean, insisted that the British aim was 'independence at the earliest possible date' and that the mission amounted to interference in Aden's domestic affairs. It was refused admission to Aden but went to Cairo and Yemen, where it naturally obtained the most adverse picture of British policy and its effects, with the result that its report described the situation as dangerous and 'likely to threaten international peace and security', and said there was a strong movement in favour of union with Yemen. It called for elections on the basis of universal adult suffrage, and alleged that there was repression by the British. All this was duly denied by the British delegates, but the General Assembly at its autumn session in 1963 demanded self-determination, the release of political prisoners, an end to repressive action, and the early removal of the British base.

This evidence of outside interest and support encouraged the opposition which was stirring again in Aden, and the incidence of political strikes increased. Big demonstrations took place in support

*Sir Charles Johnston had finished his term of service in August 1962, and had asked not to be reappointed because his wife's health could no longer stand the climate.

of the United Nations Committee when it was refused admission. The police dispersed the crowds with tear gas and arrested about a hundred demonstrators. The authorities were armed with a new law which had been one of the first acts of the federal government in January 1963, and which defined sedition as any attempt to claim or encourage others to claim that the Federation was part of any other state. This was directly aimed at the Aden TUC and its supporters who advocated union with Yemen and described the federal area as 'South Yemen'.

The National Front for the Liberation of South Yemen (NLF) was formed in Sanaa to direct resistance. Before long, Aden was full of weapons smuggled in from Yemen. The Aden government replied by imprisoning PSP and union leaders on the most suitable available charge, with the result that terrorism was so confronted by repression that the UN protest about political prisoners was justified by the facts. The Egyptian forces in Yemen had meanwhile pressed southwards to the frontier, and their presence, together with the abundance of arms in the region, encouraged all the would-be dissident tribesmen to start trouble again.

Duncan Sandys summoned the ministers of both Aden and the Federation to London in December 1963, but while they were waiting at the airport, a hand-grenade was thrown among them, fatally wounding the Assistant High Commissioner, George Henderson, and injuring Sir Kennedy Trevaskis, two of the ministers, the Reuter correspondent and some spectators. There can be little doubt that Sir Kennedy was the intended victim, for he was believed to be both architect of the merger and, from his long service in the Western Protectorate, very much a supporter of the tribal rulers against the Aden *politicos*. He happened to be only slightly hurt, and the London conference was postponed while he declared a State of Emergency and stayed at his post to oversee the counteraction, which consisted mainly of deporting about 280 Yemenis and interning fifty-seven prominent members of the PSP and the ATUC who were still at large. (They were all released by mid-February.) The Federal Supreme Council closed the frontier with Yemen (in so far as this was possible) and the Minister of the Interior ordered the registration of all aliens; these were mostly citizens of Yemen. Khalifa Abdullah Hassan al-Khalifa was arrested and charged with the murder of Henderson. (He was acquitted the following April because the main prosecution witness was in Yemen, but was immediately rearrested under the emergency regulations.)

The Aden government was unhappy about the declaration of the State of Emergency and even more disturbed when the federal government, claiming responsibility for internal security, removed the political prisoners to Fadhli sultanate whence there soon came reports of ill-treatment and even of torture. The High Commissioner did not exercise his right to intervene and Duncan Sandys told the Commons on December 19 that the High Commissioner was not 'directly responsible'. This was too much for Ali Salem Ali, who resigned once again, and it was with some difficulty that Sir Kennedy Trevaskis prevented the resignation of the entire cabinet.

II

Thus ended the first troubled year of the Federation of South Arabia, the mould from which it was intended to cast the new South Arabian state in the course of a few years. Its existence was based entirely on the understanding that British money would bolster its economy and that British forces would maintain its security for many years to come. Without this belief the tribal states would not have joined, and it would have been impossible to get the Aden ministers to press forward with the merger or form a government afterwards.

Mohammed Husseini, then Minister of Education and Information, had put the position clearly in his broadcast on September 9, 1962:

... we have felt bound to recognise the importance of Aden to the British as one of their main military bases outside the United Kingdom. We have therefore agreed with the British Government that the entry of Aden into the Federation should not affect British sovereignty over Aden or the reserved powers of the government. This is a matter where our interests and the interests of our British friends agree fully with each other. They need security of tenure for their base: we need the money that the British forces spend in Aden and which at present runs at the rate of about £11 million a year.

The Federal Supreme Council acted on the assumption that security of tenure was still the main factor; and, in the belief that public opinion at home and in the Arab world could be satisfied only by the early grant of independence, it proposed that after independence the British should hold the base on lease. The presence of Egyptian troops in Yemen had made the point all the more important to the Federation.*

They had every right to be confident. Sir Charles Johnston pressed through the merger with a firm belief in 'the underlying determination of the British Government to retain the Aden base . . .'. The London agreement provided specifically for it, even to the retention of the right to detach areas within Aden as a sovereign base area if necessary. Its continued existence was an integral part of Britain's defence policy, and this was affirmed many times by British ministers. The Defence White Paper of 1962 declared that British troops would be based 'permanently' in Aden, giving as reason the needs of global strategy, the defence of oil interests in the Persian Gulf, *and* the protection of Arab and other allies.

The external situation at the time also created a state of mind in London favourable to the Aden base. There was strife in Cyprus which seemed to endanger the British military establishment there, and Kenyan independence meant that the East African base would be evacuated. The 24th Infantry Brigade was moved from Kenya to Aden, raising the total of British forces there to 5,000 troops and 4,000 RAF personnel. The cost of the base (as distinct from the expenditure in Aden of the services and the men) was now running

---

*'In the Federation and protectorates our presence is the main assurance to the rulers of their continued existence as independent States. Their main anxiety is to see us stay and the base remain here'; K. W. Simmonds, Deputy Governor of Aden, quoted by the Special Correspondent of *The Times*, October 10, 1961.

at about £6 million a year. There was the very visible sign of large barrack blocks going up in Little Aden to confirm the permanence of British policy.

The year had closed with a demonstration of British strength in support of the Federal Regular Army, which was being trained and formed by Brigadier James Lunt, a former officer of the Jordan Arab Legion who had been sent out specially for the task. It had four battalions in service and a fifth in formation. The infiltration of armed tribesmen from Yemen intent on fomenting revolt against the Sultan of Dhala was already keeping the force on its toes, and at the end of the year two battalions had to be deployed against 1,000 Radfan tribesmen armed with rifles and grenades who emerged from their mountain passes seeking trouble. The British promptly provided artillery, helicopters, armoured cars, road engineers and RAF Hunter aircraft in support of 'Operation Nutcracker'.

The belief in British support prevented a collapse of confidence at the end of 1963. No one had expected the merger to take place without some trouble, and the degree of trouble was not much greater than expected and had been handled with a firmness that pleased the ultra-conservatives of Aden. The road to independence might be murky, but at least the British would be there to see that the traffic did not get too far out of line and would remain to see it was properly parked at the end.

There were, nevertheless, grave doubts even among people who supported federation, notably concerning the power of the federal rulers. However firmly they wanted the PSP and TUC politicians handled, they did not like the fact that they had been handed over to internment in Fadhli state, for this appeared to be a surrender by the High Commissioner to the sultans against whom the Adenis expected him to defend them. Then there had been an ominous incident when the Sultan of Fadhli brought his own armed troops to Aden airport. The situation in Aden itself was also far from satisfactory. The arrests did not stop terrorism, for a minister of Aden state was shot at by a gunman on a beach. The much disputed franchise question was still in the air after Duncan Sandys had rejected the recommendations of the all-party committee, and there were no signs of a radical reform of the Aden constitution, which Baharoon himself said needed altering 'from A to z'.

Many of the Adenis were suspicious of the role of Sir Kennedy Trevaskis, and when a group of British members of parliament visited Aden and the adjacent federal area in late December, they were handed a petition by Adeni municipal councillors asking for his removal from the office of High Commissioner. Their anxiety stemmed primarily from Sir Kennedy's excellent relations with the rulers of the Western Protectorate to whom he had been Political Agent and Adviser for many years; the councillors described him as 'a friend of the feudal sultans'. This should have been good ground for satisfaction because no one else could better influence the sultans and carry Aden's case to them, but his very detailed knowledge of the protectorates made him cautious about the concepts of a unitary state and democratic processes then being mooted. The Federation was running far ahead of the first formula he had drafted. The Adenis interpreted Trevaskis's attitude as indicating an attempt to preserve the primitive conditions and power of the protectorate states as long as possible, and not as a sincere attempt to make a difficult plan workable.

Perhaps no one knew better than the High Commissioner just what the plan entailed and the difficulties to be faced, and if he regarded the traditional values of the tribal states as a more solid foundation for policy than the inchoate theories of the Adeni politicians, this did not mean that he would not try to make the Federation work or that he would sell Aden down the river. His knowledge of the area was not, however, matched by adequate comprehension of the extent to which urban national opinion was dominant and able to influence tribal areas. Because that opinion penetrated the region by means of Radio Cairo, it was easy to conclude that it only expressed Nasser's ambition and could therefore be controlled by the firm encouragement of indigenous virtues and values. (Duncan Sandys believed so, but others to come after him in London would not.)

The unstable condition of political opinion in Aden reflected a widespread confusion about the manner by which traditional thought could be moulded to the needs of the modern world, and the effect of the Federation was to create a textbook case of this classic conflict and put Britain in the position of responsibility for determining the result. As the British were quite incapable of doing so because they were unable to control the wellsprings of national opinion, the union of Aden with the Federation of the Amirates of the South committed them to the pursuit of pragmatic solutions that were bound to be imperfect by the very nature of the case.

At the end of 1963, the problem seemed less profound: to be due simply to domestic unrest in Aden, to outside interference, and to the accidental timing of the Yemeni civil war and the involvement of Egypt in it. In compensation, there was the slow but steady progress of the Federation, which was greatly helped by the confidence of the rulers in Sir Kennedy Trevaskis. The six founder-members of the original Federation of the Amirates of the South* had, by the end of 1961, been joined by the Lahej and Lower Aulaqi sultanates, the Aqrabi sheikhdom and the Dathina confederation, and then by the Wahidi and Haushabi sultanates, and the Alawi, Muflahi, and Shaibi sheikhdoms. With Aden, this made sixteen members of the Federation of South Arabia, and when the Upper Aulaqi sultanate became a member in June 1964, the Upper Yafai sultanate was the only state of any size in the Western Protectorate still outside it. Al-Ittihad (just over the frontier north of Little Aden), on which work had begun in September 1959, was functioning as the federal capital; ministers had taken over the administration of the federal subjects, and all customs barriers had been abolished on April 1 1963.

The principal failure of the plan so far lay in the refusal of the Qaiti and Kathiri sultans of the Eastern Protectorate to have any part in it. Of the Eastern area, only the Wahidi sultanate had joined. This had been foreshadowed in the earliest stages of the discussions, when the Wahidi Sultan was animated largely by fear of subservience to the Qaitis. In 1961, he had done his best, without avail, to persuade the Qaiti and Kathiris to form an Eastern Federation

*The amirates of Beihan and Dhala, the sultanates of Lower Yafai, Fadhli and Audhali, and the Upper Aulaqi sheikhdom.

(which had been part of the original Trevaskis plan), and it was only after he had failed in this that he decided to federate with the Western states.

Sir Charles Johnston retired from South Arabia in mid-1963 in the belief that the Hadrami states could be linked to the Federation, having, as he later wrote, received indications from the Sultan's Council at Mukalla that, 'provided certain differences which the Qaiti had with the Kathiri over frontiers and the distribution of oil revenues could be settled, there would probably be no objections from the Qaiti side to both Hadrami States entering the enlarged federation'.* It was likely that the Pan-American Oil Company, which had exploration rights over 5,000 square miles of the Qaiti and Kathiri states, would discover oil; but, since the Federal Constitution stipulated that oil revenues were a state and not a federal asset, there seemed no reason why this should impede the union.

The existence of the oil agreement was evidence that a degree of understanding had been reached by the two states on both frontiers and oil revenues, because the exploration area covered areas north of Wadi Hadramaut where the frontier was determined by the traditions of tribes and not by the maps of the states. The Qaiti and Kathiri Councils had decided as early as 1959 that they would co-operate over oil without prejudice to the question of ownership, and would divide any revenues in the proportion of two to Mukalla and one to Seiyun. It was on the basis of this agreement that a joint delegation reached a broad measure of agreement with the oil company in 1961.†

The accession of the Qaiti and Kathiri sultanates was considered vital to the future of the Federation, both by the British and by most of the states in the Western region. The Qaiti sultanate of Mukalla and Shihr was by far the richest in the whole area, with an income

*Johnston, p. 169.

†It is probable that the Hadrami states could have joined the Federation without more specific settlements between them had they desired to do so, and had the British administrators been willing to allow the centuries-old fluidity of the frontier to remain unchanged.

of half a million sterling from customs; and both it and the Kathiri state still had income from their emigrants, mainly in Singapore, although this source of income had greatly diminished since the independence of the states of South-East Asia after the war. The income from customs created a difficulty of its own because the Qaitis could be expected to reduce the high tariffs on joining the Federation and would need to be compensated for the loss, which would be very much greater than the £200,000 provided by the British to compensate all the states of the existing Federation.

The real difficulty, however, lay in the attempt to make the federal structure cover the entire area of British protection, including eventually the wilder Mahra sultanate on the far eastern edge. The Hadramaut had never had a natural affinity with the Western states, and from ancient times it had had an identity separate from those peoples to the west who had drifted in and out of relations with Yemen. Being travellers and traders, the Hadramis had more connection now with the urban population of Aden, among whom could be found many of Hadrami extraction; and these tended to look back over their shoulders to the land of their birth, declaring proudly from time to time 'I am an Hadrami'.

Nor were the Qaitis and Kathiris threatened by Yemen as were the federated states. In the 1930s they had feared insurgent Saudi Arabia, but that fear had greatly diminished and there was a belt of desert about 100 miles wide defending the northern border with only two tracks to carry goods and the Mecca pilgrims to and from the Hedjaz. Whereas the Western states could be persuaded to band together for strength and British support against Yemen, the Hadramis were inclined to think they might only increase the danger to themselves by doing so, for they would be giving a new political connection to the Hadramaut valley, which had always been a separate geographical region, invaded seldom and never for long. Even British protection and advice had continued to be much more protective and advisory in the Eastern than in the Western protectorates, where British power had been more and more exerted over the years to preserve the power of the rulers or remove them if they did not fit comfortably into the political pattern. For all these reasons, the original Trevaskis plan for a separate Eastern Federation made more sense, and it was this rather than union with the existing Federation which was under consistent discussion in Mukalla and Seiyun.

III

Another attempt to get the Eastern states to join was made in 1964, when the future of the Federation was itself far from clear and the circumstances therefore against success. The pressure from Yemen was increasing—so much so that, at the end of April, R. A. Butler took the opportunity of a ministerial meeting of the Central Treaty Organisation in Washington to urge the State Department to persuade President Nasser to take his troops out of Yemen and stop bothering the British in South Arabia. The sixteen-months-old Federation was still uncertain about the next steps to be taken; in particular, how it could best advance towards independence. Aden, the richest and most sophisticated state, was still under the control of the British Colonial Office, while the others were self-governing. This anomaly required to be removed as a first step. The problem of parliamentary democracy was still not solved, for, while all the federal ministers were agreed that the system for the election of the state and federal representatives should be democratic, they were at cross-purposes about the character and timing of electoral developments. The head of state was still chosen month-by-month by rotation among members of the Federal Supreme Council: a method used by the former Federation of the Amirates of the South because it was then impossible to cross intertribal barriers in order to elect a leader for a reasonable length of time. But it was clear that this arrangement could not be retained all the way to independence. There was, finally, a firm conviction in the minds of most ministers, from the sultanates and Aden alike, that the Eastern protectorates should be brought into the Federation in order to make the independent state workable.

Duncan Sandys made one of his whirlwind tours in May 1964, and summoned a constitutional conference for the following month.

Those invited to attend were, of course, the self-elected sultans and amirs from the tribal states and the Adeni ministers who had come to office through the very limited franchise that Sandys and the High Commissioner had approved. Abdullah al-Asnaj and the People's Socialist Party were regarded by both as outside the pale of constructive discussion. Asnaj was in Cairo, talking with the Arab League and President Nasser, and this was enough to complete his damnation, even though his political complexion was already beginning to fade by comparison with that of the National Liberation Front which had just been formed in Cairo from people of Aden and the sultanates. In embryo form the NLF may well have been responsible for the attempt on the life of Sir Kennedy and the murder of his deputy, Mr George Henderson, the crime for which Asnaj and most of his associates spent some months in gaol.

The federal ministers welcomed the constitution of the conference and were happy that the talks would break the long period of uncertainty and indecision. They recognised that the Federation would need a defence agreement with Britain and were willing to agree to the continuation of the base, but even on this point there was a sharp division of opinion. The federal ministers from the outlying states wanted Britain to establish a sovereign territory on the model of Cyprus, for which the Federation as a whole would be repaid by a substantial programme of financial assistance. This did not suit the Aden ministers whose territory received the entire income from the base and who therefore favoured a leased base with all the rent going to Aden.

When the conference assembled in London, Sultan Ahmed Abdullah of Fadhli state, who was chairman of the Federal Supreme Council that month, demanded immediate independence, but Baharoon, the Aden Chief Minister, wanted a unitary state with strengthened parliamentary government and democracy before self-government and independence. Baharoon wanted to be sure of internal constitutional safeguards before trusting Aden to the federal rulers. Abdullah al-Asnaj, who was in London, warned outside the conference that the aims of the conference were only to preserve Britain's position and the power of the sultans, and for that reason would lead to disorders. Away at Al-Ittihad bombs exploded to give substance to his warnings.

The Fadhli Sultan created a sensation by disappearing from the conference, dodging about from one London hotel to another like a jack-in-the-box and then departing for Cairo, announcing at Rome en route that his state had seceded from the Federation.* In these disturbing conditions, and sustained only by the adhesion of the Upper Aulaqi sultanate, the conference moved to its final session on July 4, having agreed that the Federation should be reshaped on more democratic lines with a view to independence not later than 1968 and that there would be another conference to settle details and, above all, to negotiate a defence agreement under which Britain would retain its military base. It was also decided to renew talks with the Kathiri, Qaiti and Mahra Sultans with a view to their joining the Federation.

The outcome was a masterpiece of drafting but it did not settle the main questions, such as the form that democracy would take. The holding of elections on a wide franchise had been put forward and Asnaj wanted this applied to all the up-country states as well as Aden, arguing that the transistor radio had given even bedouin some knowledge of political issues. The conference communique referred to 'direct elections as and when practicable', which implied a gradual and varied approach. Only the Fadhli state thought that direct elections could be held more or less at once. The conference provided for commissions to advise on these elections in the states outside Aden, with male adult suffrage, but the sittings of the commission were postponed until after the Aden elections in October, largely because the Adenis were among the very few who could provide some expertise. Aden, it was agreed, would have absolute control over its internal security, but Adenis soon came to the view that this had solved nothing, for, if a federal government could delegate the right, it might also take it away if Britain were no

---

*Sultan Ahmed Abdullah was duly deposed by the Federal Supreme Council and banned from South Arabia and his successor kept the state in the Federation. He remained in Cairo for some time as one more minor thorn in the British flesh and gave his pennyworth of advice to a UN fact-finding mission.

longer able to prevent its doing so in an independent federal state. The situation in Britain was itself on the verge of change. In October 1964, the Labour Party won a narrow victory at the General Election, forming a government with Harold Wilson as Prime Minister and Anthony Greenwood in the place of Duncan Sandys. 'Aden will be the first test by which the Arabs decide whether Mr. Wilson's Government is truly of a new colour', noted *The Economist* on October 31. 'The situation demands urgency.' The new British government certainly desired to change the course of events, believing with the simplicity born in long years of exile from office that it was their predecessors' ideas and not the facts of the case that caused the difficulties. They had no intention of abandoning the Federation and, as Dennis Healey, the Minister of State, re-affirmed in November, intended to maintain the base, but they did not believe it the duty of a Labour government to preserve the power of 'feudal sultans', and were convinced that it would be possible to bring the Aden resistance movement into happy, democratic association with the federal rulers.

Sir Kennedy Trevaskis was recalled to London at the end of October to report on the situation and heard from the new Minister of State, Anthony Greenwood, of the new approach. He had little faith in the experiment. The delayed Aden Legislative Council elections had just been held on the basis of a new Act that limited the franchise to persons born in Aden. This had pleased neither the Federal Supreme Council, who considered that its narrowness encouraged the separatist tendencies in Aden, nor the opponents of the government, who considered it much too narrow. There had been explosions in Al-Ittihad and Aden which were believed to be the work of the National Front for the Liberation of South Yemen, the Cairo-backed resistance movement. The People's Socialist Party of Abdullah al-Asnaj called for a boycott.

The election was pushed through under maximum security conditions made possible by the State of Emergency; police guarded all public buildings and no public meetings were allowed, and the campaign was preceded by a widespread hunt for dissidents and a raid on the PSP headquarters. As the great majority of the PSP supporters were without the right to vote under the new franchise, the boycott had little effect, and 76 per cent of the 8,000 people entitled to vote went to the polls to return the sixteen members of the Council. Nevertheless, the PSP claimed that even on this narrow franchise they had seven sympathisers elected, one of whom was Khalifa Abdullah Hassan al-Khalifa who had been accused of the grenade outrage at the airport and was still in detention. The PSP now demanded his release from prison and appointment as Chief Minister, but Sir Kennedy, whose murder Khalifa was thought to have intended, not unnaturally ignored the demand and reappointed Baharoon.

In short, the security required for these elections—carried out while the Conservative government was still in office—did not suggest to Sir Kennedy that the time was ripe for a new democratic deal. When Greenwood arrived in Aden in November there were a number of bomb outrages in one of which two British soldiers were killed. He held talks with federal and Aden ministers and party leaders, visited the Western Protectorate, and while in Beihan witnessed for himself a full-scale Yemeni attack on Beihan. His fortnight in the region, nevertheless, seemed to give promise of success. Both the Aden and federal ministers issued a statement in favour of 'a unitary sovereign state on a sound democratic basis' and announced that a joint Ministerial Committee would meet in London in March to prepare for it. Anthony Greenwood reassured the federal government that he would provide every assistance against external aggression and internal subversion. The PSP undertook to abandon its campaign for union with Yemen.

On the face of it, the deteriorating situation had been saved. *The Times* considered the new plan as 'realistic' and described how power would remain in traditional hands whereas the unitary state would be run on democratic lines by the politicians. It envisaged the participation of the PSP, 'the best organised political movement in the area' without whose participation 'no constitutional arrangement for Aden or South Arabia as a whole can make sense'.* It was a moment of promise but not one of which Sir Kennedy Trevaskis thought highly. His premature retirement in December and the

*December 8, 1964.

appointment of Sir Richard Turnbull, former Governor General of Tanganyika, was announced.

At the end of 1964 the federal plan was far ahead of what had been intended and a unitary democratic state less than four years away. The manner and means of bringing it into existence was yet to be determined and was far more important than the concept. By what means were the Arabs of the protectorate states, some farmers, some fighting hillmen, to be brought into the same fold as the Aden townsmen or urban Arabs of Lahej? The educational standards in the tribal states were so low that only 5 per cent of the secondary school pupils in Aden came from the areas outside and this, combined with many tribal differences, friendships and enmities, gave little promise of effective democracy. The vital problem lay in bringing the outside states as close as possible and as quickly as possible to Aden's social level, yet on this point British policy seemed to have moved in the opposite direction, for the federal development plan for 1964-66 had been cut from £8 million to just over £1 million. The Federation was costing Britain more money than had ever been intended, but most of it was spent on maintaining the up-country states (for which Britain provided 86 per cent of the ordinary revenues), and on the Federal Army, which Britain maintained entirely. In short, the funds were required to get the Federation off the ground and then prop it against internal and external troubles. The British government, it is true, had now promised another £9 million, but even this was considered insufficient by the Supreme Council who throughout had emphasised the need for a massive development programme. It pointed out that, after more than a century of the British connection, there were only fourteen miles of tarmac road outside Aden and argued that if the money spent on 'Operation Nutcracker' in the Radfan area—which had dragged on for months—had been spent on development there, the campaign would never have been necessary.

VII

The haste of the London decision was doubtless made necessary by the fact that, once independence was promised, it was difficult to keep it to the slow and measured advance required by the circumstances; but the fact remained that South Arabia had been launched on a difficult and troubled four years. There were already important pointers to the future. Two of the most significant were the election to the Legislative Council of the gaoled Khalifa Abdullah Hassan al-Khalifa, widely believed to be guilty of the crime for which he could not be tried, and the emergence of the National Liberation Front (NLF).

The limited franchise on which the elections had taken place ensured the exclusion of extremists from the Council, but there could be no mistake about the election of Khalifa. It was at once a protest against the State of Emergency, against his redetention after acquittal, and against the British policy of federation in general. It gave the lie to the opinion of some British officials that only a gang of Yemenis and others brain-washed by Egypt were responsible for resistance in Aden, for the Adenis did not vote and not many of the people susceptible to the influence of Egypt were supposed to have the vote. Above all, it showed that there was a body of opinion in Aden ready to applaud terrorism.

In later years, October 1963 was to be recognised as the start of the national revolt in South Arabia; and, by October of 1964, the momentum of armed resistance was beginning to mount. Qahtan as-Shaabi had deserted the South Arabian League to become leader of the NLF, which was committed to violence from the outset. Like the other leaders of the South Arabian League, As-Shaabi was from Lahej, but he did not share the Jifris' attachment to the deposed Sultan and held much more extreme views. He had studied agriculture at Khartoum University, and even in those days of his youth his fanaticism was a byword among the Sudanese students. His new organisation drew its support mainly from the gun-slinging tribesmen upcountry who now found that membership of the NLF entitled them to rifles and sometimes automatic weapons of which there was now an abundant supply available from the Egyptian forces just over the frontier in Yemen, As-Shaabi having secured the support of the Egyptian government for armed resistance.

Abdullah al-Asnaj and his People's Socialist Party were no longer the trusted instrument of Egyptian policy. Although still regarded as an extremist in Aden government circles, he was already being condemned as too moderate by his own people and in Cairo because he believed that much could be gained and much trouble averted by negotiating with the British Labour government. As a leading trade unionist, Asnaj had had many contacts with the Labour Party and the British Trade Union Congress before the party was returned to office in 1964, and it was his trust in them which prompted his conciliatory mood during the visit of Anthony Greenwood. He had no part in the series of incidents that disturbed Aden in which two newspaper offices were burnt down and, for the first time, bazookas were used. The Egyptian government distrusted him because he made no secret of the fact that he was as little prepared to be a puppet of Egypt as of the British.

This period, when the Labour Party was newly in power in Britain, provided the second and last occasion when a radical reassessment of British policy in Aden could have been made to bring the radical Adeni groups into the federal fold. The first opportunity had slipped by in 1962 because of the desire to railroad the federal plan through the Aden Legislative Council. In 1964, it was considered impossible to offer any terms to Asnaj that could have been successfully imposed on the federal rulers, who wrongly supposed him to be the chief Egyptian instrument in South Arabia. Neither the rulers nor the Aden government then believed that the NLF resistance was a serious matter; it seemed, at the worst, no more than another tiresome security problem which could be handled in the usual way.

The situation in the tribal areas was far from happy, and in retrospect it can be seen that the seeds of the NLF revolt were already being sown. The Radfan rebellion had compelled the British government to fly a battalion of the Scottish Borderers to the region, and even with their help the rebellion was not brought under control for another three months. There were the usual ingredients of unruly tribesmen and arms and incitement from Yemen, but this time the situation was the more serious in that the NLF was working from Yemen and in collaboration with the Egyptians. There was also unrest in Dathina state, and in the Fadhli sultanate after the defection of the ruler in London. These were serious symptoms. Fadhli was relatively prosperous and was located at the heart of the federal area; Dathina was relatively sophisticated with an annually elected leader and close links with Aden through its migrant workers. In both cases there were signs of political resistance to the Federation.

It is doubtful whether Abdullah al-Asnaj could have brought much influence to bear upcountry except perhaps on workers who had connections with Aden. Officials in Aden held that it would have been impossible in any case to find terms that Asnaj would have accepted. There was, however, one element in the situation that might have justified a sustained effort to bring him in. This was the conflict between Qahtan as-Shaabi's group and Asnaj, for it was the beginning of the struggle for power among the extremists which was destined to bring Aden to near-ruin. The political scene in the Colony had always been dominated by individuals and groups jockeying for power, but as long as the British were the dispensers of power the consequences were seldom serious. The internal political struggle was now different, for the long-term intention of each contestant was to secure power when the British departed. Qahtan as-Shaabi pinned his faith on open rebellion, whereas at this stage Asnaj was hoping to negotiate himself into the position of inheritor of British authority. As it became clear that Asnaj's hope could not be fulfilled, the optimism generated by Greenwood's visit to South Arabia was seen to be false. The stage was thus set for the bloodshed and disorder which characterised the remaining period of South Arabia's advance to independence.

6

The Embryo State

THE FEDERATION established the shape of a unitary independent state of South Arabia. If the Eastern Protectorate joined, its population would be substantially increased and its area more than doubled, and it would include the fertile Hadramaut valley. But there were no signs that this would happen. At the end of 1964, therefore, the embryo state presented a picture of overwhelming poverty relieved only by the prosperity of Aden itself.

I

The Aden Colony, which was all that British history in South Arabia had been about for 130 years, was an area of only 75 square miles, enclosing a bay guarded by two promontories of jagged volcanic rock so harsh that at sunrise, sunset or moon-time they had a satanic beauty. The visitor coming from the sea saw only a repellent barrenness of yellow sands shading to black in the sharp ridges of the hills, without vegetation or any softness to relieve the scene. For most of the year a heavy heat weighed upon it, and its inhabitants breathed from the sea.

Arabs fished in the shallow waters of the coast from small boats, or waded on foot with handnets which they threw swirling over the water. On the lowland behind the bay there were pans where the sea evaporated to deposit its salt. Aden had no other natural wealth except that derived from its position on the routes from the Mediterranean and Africa to the East. It was by nurturing its value as a bunkering port for ships that the British raised it from a fishing village to one of the greatest ports in the world. When the importance of coal declined as a fuel, they brought in oil, and a refinery and storage tanks were built on the sheltered inner shore of the Western Promontory. Around this oil depot grew up a new town, Little Aden.

Aden town proper is known as Crater because it lies inside the dead volcano bowl of the Eastern Promontory, close to the eastern shore where the enclosing ridge opens to the Arabian Sea. The main road out of the town is cut through the northern rim, a narrow gap between cliffs of rock where it bifurcates. One route passes round the northern shore through the Maala area, past the docks, through Tawahi and the complex of government and army houses, until it comes to a dead-end under the slopes of the Shamsan mountain on the south-eastern side. The other goes almost due north to the military town and airport at Khormaksar and on to the town of Sheikh Othman, crossing the frontier into the village of Dar Saad. South of Sheikh Othman a branch turns westwards through the saltpans to the new capital and then, passing more saltpans, crosses a causeway into Bureika, or Little Aden, the oil town.

Apart from some desert to the north-west, this was the entire area of the Aden Colony. Sheikh Othman is an old Arab village which has grown over the past century into a small town of low Arab houses. Crater is the Arab town with its *suk* of narrow streets but now with some villas on the eastern bay and a central block of modern buildings where banks and European business firms have their offices. In Maala, the Arab town under the hills is sheltered from public view by two streets of modern flats, one of which was still in process of construction in 1964 to meet the needs of British troops and their families. Tawahi is better known as Steamer Point, for it is here that passengers and crews come ashore from the ships bunkering in the harbour to do their shopping in a crescent of duty-free shops, behind which lies another complex of narrow shopping streets. To the west, past the Aden government offices, the British High Commissioner and Commander-in-Chief and senior British officials and officers lived until independence in houses perched on a group of low hills at Tarshyne Point. Between 1952 and 1954, Little Aden was constructed at a cost of £45 million on

270 acres of rock and sand and 200 acres recovered from the sea, and has a township to house the workers at the refinery.

The oil refineries and the port and entrepôt trade provide the principal wealth of Aden, but in 1964 there was still the considerable wealth derived from the British troops based in the Colony. About half a million tons of salt are sold from the solar-evaporation pans, and there is a small but steady income from inshore fishing. There are also many small factories which came into existence to meet the needs of the expanding population, producing soap, pots and pans, cigarettes, aluminium, dyed and printed cotton and soft drinks. There is also a mill for crushing oil-seeds. Many people are employed for the re-export trade in cleaning, sorting and packing coffee, skins, hides, oyster shell, gums and incense.

Aden was still a thriving place in 1964, and British aid in so confined an area, and controlled by British officials themselves, had rendered considerable improvement. Just over £6 million had been spent since 1955, nearly one-third of it on the social services and almost another third on housing. Over a million pounds had been spent on the public utilities. It is evidence of the prosperous condition of the Colony that about three-quarters of the labour force came from upcountry, mainly from Yemen but some from the Protectorate states. Fifteen per cent of the total labour force was employed in port activities, there was a large number of workers in Little Aden and the British camps and, because Aden was a free port and the market for all the surrounding territories, including Yemen, very many people were employed in the retail trade. The population was estimated to be about 250,000.

The importance of Aden increased rapidly after the invention of the steamship, and in 1888 a Port Trust was formed to take charge of all the activities of the harbour. By 1964, only London, Liverpool and New York surpassed it in the bunkering trade, with about 6,000 ships of nearly 30 million net registered tonnage using the port to take on fuel and fresh water. Coal steadily gave way to oil over the years and the British Petroleum storage tanks and then the refinery were meeting all the needs from 1954 onwards. In that year the Port Trust began a £3½ million development programme to make the harbour more fit to serve the larger ships on the sea routes. New quays and wharves were constructed and acres of the sea bed dredged. The old wharf, built for dhows, which were fast disappearing, was reconstructed to take bigger power-driven coastal boats, and the dredged spoil was used to reclaim 180 acres of much-needed land. The dogleg entrance channel, two miles long and 600 yards wide, and the 291 acres of the main inner harbour, were both dredged to a depth of 36 feet. To the east of it, two other areas of 74 and 73 acres respectively were dredged to 30 and 18 feet, and from the south-eastern end of the latter a channel 200 feet wide was cut to the new quay for the home trade, once the dhow wharf, at Maala. Across the bay at Little Aden, the harbour was already 40 feet deep and could take ships of 42,000 tons dead weight. In the inner harbour, there were eighteen first-class berths for ships of varying draught from 37 feet to 28 feet, and four second-class berths for ships not exceeding 16 feet draft. Ample anchorage for smaller ships existed in the area dredged to 18 feet. There was considerable enlargement of the transit and storage sheds.

The population of the Colony was extremely mixed. It had increased rapidly over a decade and there were no accurate census figures for 1964, but the 1955 census gave a clear picture of the nationalities composing it. There were 36,910 Adeni Arabs, 18,991 Protectorate Arabs, 48,088 Yemenis, 15,817 Indians and Pakistanis, 10,611 Somalis, 3,763 British, 721 other Europeans, 831 Jews and 2,608 others, including Palestinians, Syrians, Lebanese, other Arabs and Americans. There was no question that the proportion of Yemeni and Protectorate Arabs had greatly increased since the 1955 census.

One major change of population had taken place in the preceding decade, when about 7,000 Jews left Aden for Israel after the Palestine war. Some of these families may have been descended from the Jews who came to South Arabia after the destruction of Jerusalem by Titus in AD 70. They were particularly connected with craftwork in gold and silver, and lived together in a quarter of the town a little distance from the Arabs and usually at peace with them. But they were despised by the Arabs, whom they feared, and on rare occasions a small incident could cause trouble, the most notable of which was in 1931, when a quarrel over a Jewish girl's determination to marry a Muslim led to serious riots in which a number of Jews were killed and part of their quarter razed.

Tensions were never far from the surface among the communities, the Arabs, the Jews, the Indians and the Somalis. Ill-will was possibly greatest between the Arabs and the Indians and Pakistanis because of the favoured position the latter had always enjoyed under the Bombay Presidency and still enjoyed under the colonial government of Aden. Their long monopoly of the legal profession did nothing to endear them to the Arabs, who felt that they were at the mercy of these foreigners before the law. After the exodus of most of the Jewish people, the Indians were the main target of Arab dislike. Over the years, outbreaks of violence between the communities were infrequent, but when they did occur they tended to spread from one community to the other. This undertow of communal unrest was a principal cause of a great deal of the passion that infected the franchise question, for the Adenis were not so much concerned about the rights of the Yemenis and Protectorate Arabs as incensed at what seemed the unfair privileges of foreigners.

The communities maintained their languages in private or aided schools which provided education in Urdu, Hebrew and Gujarati, and in English. There were also the traditional schools at which Muslim children were given a Koranic education. After 1960, free education for children born in the Colony was provided by the government, which maintained eighteen schools, subsidised twenty-four others, and provided a technical institute and two schools for training teachers. Aden College (which had absorbed the first primary school in Aden, the College for the Sons of the Chiefs) gave academic secondary education for boys from both the Colony and the Protectorate, and provision was made for its more able pupils to continue their studies in England. The teaching was in Arabic in the primary and intermediate schools, and in English in the secondary schools.

A free government health service was also started in the Colony in 1960, largely made possible by the greatly improved hospital conditions since 1956, when the civil hospital with 350 beds was opened in Crater. There was also a civil hospital in Khormaksar and the older Church of England Mission Hospital in Sheikh Othman. Improved conditions were making some headway against the mortality rate due to tuberculosis, which was a major problem. This disease was not entirely due to overcrowding, unsanitary conditions and malnutrition; the mild narcotic *qat* enabled the chewer to go without sleep for long periods and often to increase income by doing two jobs each day, and this damaged the health of many young men. The water supply, which came from boreholes in Sheikh Othman, was of good quality but contamination of food was widespread. The birth rate was twice as high as the death rate, but both were increasing. The infant mortality rate was rising sharply, although for ten years up to 1952 it had been declining. The adverse swing was due largely to overcrowding caused by the increase of the population by both natural means and immigration.

Measured against the long period of colonial rule, the British had little to boast of in either health or education, but by 1964 the situation was showing steady improvement towards reasonable standards of social welfare and training. Aden, moreover, was far in advance of the surrounding tribal areas (which Britain advised and protected but did not rule) and Yemen and most other parts of the Arabian peninsula. Government receipts and expenditure had risen from under £3 million in 1955–56 to over £5 million in 1964. There was an efficient British-directed civil service, a trustworthy judicial system and police, and, above all, a highly efficient port system which guaranteed the prosperity of Aden in normal times.

Therefore, whatever the shortcomings of the colonial system, Adenis recognised that they had progressed far beyond all nearby territories and were jealous to guard their advantages in the Federation. On the other hand, Aden was for the Federation a profitable port and commercial capital, which, if properly cared for, could greatly ease the way to independence.

II

The Aden Information Department said of the tribal areas that composed the rest of the Federation: 'In itself this largely barren land has little to commend it and could support relatively few inhabitants.'* About 500,000 people live in this largely barren land, and those who do not travel down to Aden for work eke out miserable existencies made tolerable only by the habit of countless generations and the anarchical freedom which suits their temperament. Although only one per cent of the land can be cultivated, 90 per cent of the inhabitants live from agriculture. The remaining 10 per cent are engaged in fishing, weaving, dyeing, and the preparation of hides and skins. Even in these settled occupations, they remain tribal in character, true to their clans, and always with enmity and feuds close at hand, so that every man who can obtain a gun by purchase, gift or theft goes armed from his early youth. The frontier between loyalty and rebellion is always fragile.

They are mostly hill people. The uncomfortable coastal plain, with its humid heat, high winds and sandstorms, varies from four to ten miles in depth but contains some good, irrigated territory. It gives way inland to the low maritime range which rises about 2,000 feet above sea-level and then falls away only to climb again another 1,000 feet to the intramontane plains. On the north-east of these plains rises the highland plateau, ranging from 5,000 feet to its ridge tops at 8,000 feet, which tumbles roughly 6,000 feet into the sands of the *Rub al-Khali*, the 'empty quarter' of Arabia. The landscape is harsh, characterised by sharp rocky ranges and spurs, and dissected by arid valleys cut deep into the land, usually with precipitous sides and with very little vegetation.

The people live in small pockets widely scattered over the highlands wherever they can cultivate alluvial terraces, or on the flat beds of wadis where the winter flood-water can be retained, or near hills where the winter flood-water can be channelled into tanks and cisterns. Millet is the chief cereal, but they also grow some barley and wheat, together with some castor oil, indigo and tobacco. Down

---

*This hand-out (dated June 18, 1961) continues: 'It is due both to the ingenuity of its people and the development schemes now in progress that the difficulties of the environment do not seriously impede *its economic prosperity*.' The italics are mine. To speak of prosperity in the poverty-stricken region outside Aden was misleading to any stranger reading the hand-out.

at the coast, British help and money have made cotton an important crop in Lahej and in the Abyan area of the Fadhli and Lower Yafa sultanates. These areas also have date palms, sago palms and the mango, paw-paw, banana and guava trees.

For nearly a century, the Arabs of this area and the British lived in mutual toleration by taking as little notice of each other as possible. The British were content to leave the tribesmen to themselves until banditry became too troublesome on any particular caravan route or the ruler of one of the states too tiresome. It was, in any case, very difficult to do very much in such rough country, where tribesmen as agile as mountain goats and knowing every rock and cranny could vanish at will. The situation only changed radically when rugged trucks with four-wheel drives could invade the fastnesses; and it was finally transformed when aeroplanes could seek and punish offenders at speed and with impunity. It was not until after the First World War that the Aden government found it practicable to concern itself more closely with the affairs of the tribes; and at the same time, or because of it, the British began to develop a conscience about them. The advisory treaties were symptomatic of the change.

It was not easy to develop land communications. The tribesmen were not enthusiastic for roads—vehicular traffic might damage their caravan trade or perhaps bring punitive troops—and they were inclined to dig them up again if they had the chance. The territory made almost every mile of road an engineering feat. The Tirah Pass road between Lodar and Mukeiras in the Audhali sultanate required, in the first place, the cutting of six miles into the side of a near-vertical cliff, rising through a series of forty-five hairpin bends over precipice after precipice to the Mukeiras plateau at 7,400 feet. If there was not a great deal to show in the development of ground communications this was largely because there was no trade to justify the vast expense involved in making an adequate road network, and no one could, or can, visualise a state wealthy enough to maintain the network if it were built. By 1959, however, there was a motor road and track connecting Aden with Lahej and passing through Wadi Tiban to Taiz in Yemen to carry the trade between the port and that country; and another motorable route went from Aden through Abyan area, the Fadhli, Dathina and Aulaqi territories to Beihan, tortuously going east to get north. These roads or improved tracks were perhaps all that was necessary. One could get to most places of any importance, but it was usually a very rough ride; and the camel had still its *raison d'être*.

Meanwhile, the aeroplane was also playing its part, particularly in the movement of people and mail. Landing strips were laid down in almost all sizeable centres of population, and Aden Airways built up an internal service which enabled people to move between the main centres and Aden, often taking less than an hour for a journey which, by routes over rugged territory, could take days. This was of supreme value to the Governor of Aden, who was able to keep much better contact with the rulers and his agents and advisers in the field. Air transport also helped the health service greatly, making it possible to convey from Protectorate areas to the hospital at Aden emergency cases which, in earlier days, were liable to be dead before they got there.

A major result of British concern for the tribes was the creation of rudimentary social services, one of which was the Protectorate health service, which worked to create a standardised system throughout the tribal area, largely with British money. The health service also secured outside help from the Nuffield Foundation, which provided materials for medical education, and from UNICEF, which was particularly helpful in maternity and child welfare. The principal purposes of the service were to train medical staff, advise the states on their own health work, and allocate the money from the Colonial Development and Welfare Fund. It came under a British health adviser, who directed the British work and advised the states. Six hospitals were built at strategic points in the Protectorate, but advanced medical treatment had to be given in Aden.

Education had also progressed under the direction of the Director of Education of Aden Colony. By 1964, there were 120 small primary schools, two intermediate schools and one junior secondary school; and Britain was financing the teachers and the entire cost of the intermediate and secondary schools. Promising students then continued their studies at Aden College, and those with marked ability were sent to England.

Progress was inevitably limited in such a primitive society. Some rulers and their families were anxious to help, but even when they were prepared to be generous, they were not wealthy enough to do much. The result was that almost everywhere the advances depended on British money and, often, pressure. Without British initiative and the modest sums provided, it is doubtful whether there would have been any progress at all. The general poverty of the region constituted the main problem, and this was extremely difficult to change. The Department of Agriculture in Aden did what it could with the funds available, and successive Governors and High Commissioners pleaded with London for more; but it was not until the prospect and reality of federation made it plain that much more money was required that a major effort seemed possible. The results, nevertheless, were very modest by 1964.

The Department of Agriculture helped with advice, training and money wherever it could. Its most ambitious and successful project by far was the Abyan scheme, which covered 120,000 acres straddling the border of the Fadhli and Lower Yafa sultanates. Here the coastal area has unusually rich soil, yielding vegetables, fruit and cotton. The scheme was launched with a loan of £270,000 from the Colonial Development and Welfare Fund, the aim being to invest a million pounds out of profits to develop the region fully. Within ten years, the Abyan Board and the preceding administration which ran the scheme had spent £1½ million, all from its surpluses. The Abyan Board was by far the biggest organisation in Yafa, taking over from an administration of Aden government employees who had run the scheme for the first seven years. Consisting of twelve members from the Fadhli and Yafa states, it became a supreme authority, divorced entirely from the Aden government unless it chose to ask for advice or help. It supervised the cultivation of cotton and marketed it throughout the world. Over the years, it had greatly extended and improved the old irrigation system by building a dam to store water in Wadi Bana and two main trunk canals to feed water to the network of smaller irrigation channels.

With these works went many other essential developments, such as roads and transport, reserve electricity supplies, a ginning factory and warehouses. The total effect was greatly to improve the standard of living in the area, and the population increased tenfold in ten years.

Lower Yafa was a most advanced country by South Arabian standards. The young Sultan, Mahmud bin Aidrus, ruled through his Naib and a state council of sixteen appointed members, and with an administration of fourteen departments and a state treasury that was unusual in keeping proper accounts. The Lower Yafa sultanate spent about £16,000 a year on education, providing primary schools (including one for girls) and an excellent intermediate school from which pupils could qualify for entrance to Aden College. Its annual expenditure also included £7,000 on health services and £12,000 on development. The income of the state was £100,000 a year. Of this, £40,000 was spent on the ruling family, the tribes and the traditional hospitality to visitors. This high proportion for what apparently was a privy purse was not totally unreasonable, for a complicated system of 'local government' was maintained throughout the five provinces by the sheikhs of the tribes, on whom the security of the state and the roads in some measure depended, and they were paid for their services.

Not all Protectorate states had an organisation worthy of the name. It was enough that the ruling family elected its head and secured the approval of the tribal sheikhs; thereafter, the tribal ruler selected a close relative as his Naib and together they ruled the state in complete authority, limited only by custom which sometimes imposed consultation. Lahej, the state closest to Aden and the richest, had a more sophisticated manner of choosing its ruler, which was somewhat akin to an electoral college; but the choice was limited to the Abdali family. It had also a relatively sophisticated government system. To the north-west, there was the Dathina confederation of tribes, organised as such by the British because there was no means of apportioning them to neighbouring states; and this had a quite abnormal council system, with the chairmanship rotating among the sheikhs of the participating tribes.

To a large extent, the form of state government was advanced or retarded in accordance with geography, the accessibility to Aden and the extent to which the rulers could control the hill country. The British themselves had had little contact with the Lower Yafa hills until after the Second World War, and some parts of the Fadhli state close to Aden were hardly penetrated at all. Cultivated valleys in plateaux—such as that at Beihan—were scattered about the region, but many of them were cut off by difficult mountainous territory. There were thus great differences, not only between states, but within tribes within states: between the Yafa voyagers who went far afield and the nomads of Beihan in their black tents, or, more simply, between the man who tended his fields on irrigated land and his near neighbour who wandered with his flocks in the hills in search of grazing land. Inevitably, there were innumerable enmities and feuds between ruling families and within tribes and families, and to these were added the frontier troubles besetting the states bordering on Yemen.

The Tribal Levies, later to become the Federal Army, which had for years helped to keep the peace, were largely composed of Audhali and Aulaqi tribesmen. They had become almost a separate population group (their training, education and discipline setting them apart from most of their fellows), but they were still too close to their origins to forget for a moment their ultimate tribal loyalties. Their loyalty was never questioned; they were simple, good fellows, it was said, who were proud of themselves as uniformed military men. Yet it was inevitable that some of the Britishness of their environment would rub off on them, and they would draw unfavourable comparisons between the organisation they admired and the conditions back home. Young officers would speak unfavourably of tribal justice and the need to apply the Aden judicial system in the federal areas outside—which was not, on the face of it, a very revolutionary idea, but it reflected their desire for change. They were also affected by the propaganda from Egypt and Yemen, which was often aimed directly at them as soldiers who were sustaining British rule.

This propaganda also had its impact on the more advanced towns of the region, such as Lahej, Zinjibar and Jaar, which were notably in areas where cotton-growing had created new standards of living. For wealth, even though only relative to conditions a few years earlier, was itself a revolutionary influence, and this influence increased with the amount of education provided for the people. From the late fifties onwards, it was common enough to see pictures of President Nasser in coastal and upcountry towns, and sometimes an Englishman was greeted by crowds chanting the Egyptian leader's name.

It might well be that, by 1964, many of the rulers, such as those of Lahej, Fadhli, Yafa and Dhala territories, were aware that the seeds of Arab nationalism of the Nasser variety had been sown widely through federal territory; but if they were, they had not conveyed their awareness successfully to the British on whom they relied for their security. The Aden government seemed to regard political insurgence as an exclusive characteristic of the Colony and the strength of the outside rulers as a defence against it.

III

While the British were only beginning to realise the difficulty of constructing a state in South Arabia, the Egyptians were already well-advanced in knowledge of the problem they had set themselves in trying to remould the ancient kingdom of Yemen into a modern republic. Although Yemen had a long history of central authority, its geographical and tribal conditions presented major obstacles to a successful war.

The western and southern parts of Yemen have fertile plains, the north is mountainous and the east is desert. The people of the west and south were able to make passable livelihoods as farmers and traders, and were not dependent on the pecuniary help of the Imam or the sheikhs. Moreover, because they were more directly under the control of the Imam, they resented his arbitrary authority. This was not true of the hillmen and desert nomads. The sheikhs lived on terms of oral truce with him and depended sometimes on his bounty, while the tribesmen in turn depended for their well-being on the sheikhs. When the royalist forces began to resist in the north, they were able to use Saudi Arabian money to subsidise their tribal supporters. These conditions established the broad division between republicans in the west and south and the royalists in the north and east. Republican allegiance was further strengthened by the resistance of the Shafei Muslims, mainly in the east, to the Zeidi royalists.

The picture was, in detail, even more complicated. The great Hashid and Bakil tribal confederations were mainly from the north and could possibly have determined the issue if their 130,000 warriors had all been committed to one side, but they were not. The paramount sheikh of the Hashid, the young Abdullah bin Hussein al-Ahmar, was republican because his father and brother had both been executed by the late Imam Ahmed, and some of the tribes in his confederation followed him into the republican camp while others remained royalist. This kind of division was also evident in the even greater Bakil confederation. Of the Banat Shaker's seven subtribes, all were royalist except one, the Dugheilan. Similarly, the Kholan group had six royalist clans and one republican. The Daham, Naham and Arhab tribes were royalist, but the Sufian, Murhaba and Bani Matar were republican. These allegiances could change. Republican tribes could be bought with Saudi money or could swing against the republicans if offended by a high-handed Egyptian action. The Egyptians and republicans could count more heads on their side because the areas they controlled had the larger share of the population, but their hold was never firm.

The republican system of government was not easily understood by the Yemenis, who were accustomed to the theocratic rule of the Imam, which they could resent but still accept as traditional. Under the Imam, the germ of civil government existed in the Amils, or district officers, who directed the local civil law. There was the right of appeal to the district councils, but the final court of appeal was the Imam himself. Personal status was judged by the Sharia, or Koranic, law, but over a great part of the country tribal law still survived. The rate of literacy was high in Sanaa, where there were several schools and a low-grade university, and in the provincial centres there were also schools; but over most of the country education was limited to Koranic recitation. There was a

133

F

rudimentary system of taxation imposed by the Imam, who had translated almsgiving as prescribed by the Koran into fixed payments to the state or, in the case of poor peasants, as manual labour on the rock-surfaced roads.

The power of chieftains was still considerable in their own districts, which they ruled from the towns. With narrow streets, open sewers and high houses, usually enclosed with strong walls several hundreds of years old and protected by a citadel, these were strongholds from which the chieftains could dominate the surrounding country. Their loyalty to any cause was unreliable and governed by their own interests; and even the army, which was about 20,000 strong, could not be relied on because of the tribal affiliations of the troops. In effect, therefore, the rudimentary government was imposed through the chieftains who, in turn, were responsible to the Imam. The centralised government which the republicans were trying to construct was foreign to the people and damaging to the chieftains.

Egyptian soldiers and officials worked hard to construct a new administration with the help of Yemenis (who were much less qualified than the people the Aden government had at its disposal in the Federation), and they hastened to make material improvements in Sanaa and Taiz which would give visible evidence of the brave new world ahead. Some places benefited in the natural course of events, notably Hodeida. This port had little trade (most of which went through Aden) until Russians, Chinese and Egyptians used it; moreover, it was undisturbed by the royalists.

These constructive efforts were frustrated in a large measure by the instability of the republican government. Not only were there quarrels early in 1963 between Sallal and his able deputy, Abdul Rahman Baidani, but there were already signs of discontent in the cabinet over the heavy-handed Egyptian occupation. Baidani himself soon suffered eclipse. He flew to Cairo on January 27, 1963 to protest to President Nasser against Sallal's handling of the situation. When he failed to get satisfaction, he went on to Aden for the ostensible purpose of establishing a Yemen Development Bank, and was thereupon deprived of Yemeni citizenship in August 1963.

A month later, he returned to Cairo to try to put the matter right and was promptly put under house arrest. Baidani's protest in January nevertheless stirred the Egyptian government to action, and Field Marshal Abdel Hakim Amer and Colonel Anwar Sadat, Minister for Yemeni Affairs, flew to Sanaa where they arranged for a new government and presidential council 'to provide collective rule'. Sallal's position was strengthened by his taking over the portfolio of Minister of Foreign Affairs which Baidani had held.

In January 1964, Sallal made a new effort to establish a constitutional government and at the same time to increase his power. The new organs of government were a nine-man Political Bureau and a National Security Council, but he also declared himself head of state, chairman of both organs and commander-in-chief. A month later, he appointed an Executive Council, proposed the formation of a Yemen Progressive Union on the pattern of the Egyptian Arab Socialist Union, and appointed a military board charged with the task of building a strong national army, together with a currency board authorised to issue paper money to replace the Maria Theresa dollar then in circulation.

Apart from the paper money, which appeared immediately, none of these organisations functioned successfully, and the whole scheme caused a great deal of discontent among leading republicans. In April 1964, President Nasser made his first visit to Yemen to put matters right. The result was yet another constitution, with a President (Sallal), a Prime Minister, a Consultative Council, a National Defence Council, a judiciary and municipalities. General Hamud al-Gayefi, a 'strong man' who was yet thought capable of reconciling differences within the republican fold, became Prime Minister in May; and Nasser kept Sallal on visits to Cairo, Russia and Pekin to give the government a chance to settle down. There was already, however, serious divergence between those who wanted the Egyptians to force a military victory and those who wanted peace talks with the royalists and the departure of the Egyptians. This gap could not easily be bridged.

The war was not going at all well. The royalists had the support of many warlike mountain tribes who were financed and armed from

Saudi Arabia. When they ran short of arms, they captured them by ambushing Egyptian columns. It was clear that their ability to keep in the field was encouraging hesitant tribes to join them, and there was sufficient support for the royalists on the central plateau for units of their forces to establish themselves for days at a time only fifteen miles outside Sanaa. They could not conquer the Egyptian forces, which numbered 40,000 men by the end of 1963, but neither could the Egyptians hold positions in the mountains. The Egyptians waged a major offensive from June to September 1963, and made considerable gains but they were quite incapable of consolidating them. It was stalemate.

The United Nations and the Arab states made efforts, without avail, to end the war. After a mission by his assistant, Ralph Bunche, U Thant reported on June 29, 1963 that he had received messages from Yemen, Saudi Arabia and Egypt agreeing to end hostilities, and a UN team of 200 observers under General Carl van Horn was sent out to supervise the disengagement. The team was quite inadequate to the task and General van Horn resigned in September when it became obvious that disengagement was neither taking place nor intended.

Prince Feisal, then Prime Minister of Saudi Arabia, had proposed in January 1963 that all intervention in Yemen—that is, his own and Nasser's—should cease and that Yemen be left to solve its own problems. But he had received no response. In the following January, a conference of Arab heads of state called for a new effort for peace. This time, Nasser, who had himself summoned the meeting for the purpose of ending inter-Arab quarrels, could not refuse. In September 1964, the two leaders met in Alexandria, where they agreed 'to work for peace in Yemen'. Feisal, however, did not recognise the republican regime, and five days after the meeting he sent a message to Imam Mohammed al-Badr congratulating him on the anniversary of his ascent to the throne.

The divergences in the republican camp came to the surface towards the end of 1964 in the emergence of a 'third force' which represented those elements seeking peace. By its efforts, a meeting took place with the royalists at Erkwit in the Sudan on November 8, when it was agreed that a peace conference would be held three weeks later. But the 'doves' of Sanaa were unable to persuade either their own 'hawks' or the Egyptian government to agree to the presence of members of the royal family at the conference, and it did not take place. There were also some tribal objections to any talks before the Egyptians completely withdrew.

The presence of Egyptian troops and the plethora of arms on the frontier inevitably led to more trouble with the Federation. The British replied with air strikes, which led Sallal to complain to the United Nations of 'flagrant aggression'. The British Legation was told to leave Taiz in February 1963 because Britain had not recognised the republican regime. After months had passed with intermittent incidents on the frontier, Britain proposed in November that a peace zone should be established to prevent them, but this was coldly received.

Egyptian intelligence officers based on Taiz were already working with the newly formed National Liberation Front to organise armed resistance in the Federation, and when President Nasser paid his visit to Yemen in April 1964, he swore 'to expel the British from all parts of the Arab world'. Although it was not known at the time, the NLF had helped to promote the large-scale Radfan rebellion which was still in progress when Nasser spoke.

The Radfan revolt is regarded by the NLF as the start of armed struggle and its birth as a formal revolutionary movement. The manner in which its small political and fighting cadres, led by 'Ali Antar' (the guerrilla name for Mohammed Nasser al-Bishi), welded dissident tribesmen, anti-sultan elements and Egyptian arms and money into a force that sustained for months South Arabia's biggest rebellion, was a significant portent for the future. It was only by putting 2,000 more troops into Aden that Britain eventually suppressed the rebellion. The outstanding success of the NLF in this campaign was to keep its part so secret that it was able to pursue undisturbed its subversive work in the tribal areas. Its clandestine organisation was so good that it was not outlawed until 1965; indeed, it was regarded by the High Commission simply as a gang of assassins until late in 1966.

Britain and Egypt were committed to the same error; one was being driven to impose a federation by force in South Arabia, and the other to establish a republic by force in Yemen. When they both decided to withdraw their troops, it was in the certain knowledge that the results would be entirely different from what they intended. It was, indeed, possible that the Federation would be to the liking of Egypt and that Yemen would, in the end, be more to the liking of the British than ever they expected.

7

The Downward Path

THE TASK facing Britain at the beginning of 1965 was to persuade the Adeni and other federal ministers to agree on the stages required to bring South Arabia to independence in 1968 and on the constitutional form of the unitary state which would then replace the Federation. It was also hoped that organisations outside the Aden government, notably the People's Socialist Party, would accept the arrangements or would come to accept them as the creation of the new state progressed.

I

In an atmosphere of increasing violence inside and outside Aden, the Colonial Secretary summoned a constitutional conference to take place in London on March 2, 1965. It was obvious that there would be difficulties over the guarantees required by Britain for the retention of the base in Aden and between the Adenis and the federal rulers over the form of the constitution. But it was for an entirely different reason that the conference never took place.

This was a demand by the federal government and Asnaj that the Eastern Protectorate states (the Qaiti, Kathiri and Mahra sultanates), which had not joined the Federation, should be invited to take part in the conference. The federal rulers and the Adeni ministers both wanted to strengthen the eventual independent state of South Arabia by bringing in the Qaiti and Kathiri sultanates in particular because their territories and population would complete it, but more especially because of their greater wealth and the prospect of increasing income from oil. It was also in the mind of the rulers that the three sultans would help to weight the tribal areas against the Adeni politicians, which would be of even more importance to them in a unitary state than in a federation.

It was, nevertheless, the Adeni ministers who precipitated the crisis by proposing to issue a strongly worded statement on behalf of their state government calling for the participation of the Eastern states. The British government and the High Commissioner saw endless difficulties in this proposal. None of the three Eastern sultanates had taken part in the complicated negotiations preceding the Aden merger or in London afterwards, and a great deal of the old ground would inevitably need to be ploughed again if they entered the discussions at this more difficult stage. The High Commissioner therefore banned the statement, whereupon the Chief Minister, Zein Baharoon, resigned and Anthony Greenwood was compelled, on February 25, to postpone the conference.

The prospect that the federal plan might be approved by the opposition was already fading rapidly under the impact of events in Cairo, where Abdullah al-Asnaj was now actively and openly working with the Egyptian government to unite the resistance movements under its wing. In February 1965, he formed the Organisation for the Liberation of the Occupied South (OLOS) by amalgamating his own People's Socialist Party with the South Arabian League* and another small party known as the Committee for the Liberation of the Occupied South. This new organisation also included some of the exiles, notably the ex-Sultan Ali Abdel Kerim of Lahej, and ex-Sultan Ahmed bin Abdullah al-Fadhli.

At the same time, the South Arabian Committee of the Arab League brought OLOS together with the extreme militant NLF in an attempt to unify all resistance. The committee consisted of Saudi Arabia, Kuwait, Tunisia, the United Arab Republic and Yemen. By a vote of three against the UAR and Yemen, it recommended that an attempt should be made to seek a political settlement with Britain without demanding prior conditions that Britain was bound to refuse. This moderate course was rejected by the NLF, in which it

---

*The SAL was soon expelled for failing to dissolve itself.

had the full support of Nasser and Sallal. Hence, the conference's decision not to rule out the possibility of achieving liberation by constitutional means had little practical effect on the situation. (The terms would in any case have been totally unacceptable to the tribal rulers. Two years later, the British government would have been glad to accept them; but in early 1965 the situation did not seem so desperate then or the rulers so feckless.) Despite this one reasonable note, it was clear that Abdullah al-Asnaj was himself moving nearer to violence, if for no other reason than his dependence on Egypt, which advocated it.

To replace Baharoon as Prime Minister of the Aden government, the High Commissioner selected Abdel Qawee Mackawee, an opposition politician who was regarded as middle-of-the-road and therefore, it was presumed, a potential bridge to more extreme people. As publicity director of the biggest firm in Aden, A. B. Besse and Company, he held what was possibly the highest position in commerce occupied by any Adeni, and this might have been expected to give him a bent for collaboration. But the position was no longer easy for an Adeni in power, particularly for one of the opposition who could be accused of going over to the other side, for death was the sanction used against them increasingly. A cleverer man would have refused the position, but Mackawee accepted it and sought to impose a 'nationalist' policy on the British government and the tribal rulers. Within a month of taking office he dissociated himself from the curfew imposed against terrorism, and he was soon demanding an end to the State of Emergency in Aden, the release of all detainees, the restoration of public freedom, self-determination on the basis of adult suffrage, the formation of a provisional government (i.e., not the existing federal government) to negotiate the date for independence, and negotiations over the military base.

The British plodded along with Mackawee, a minister totally opposed to their policy. Denis Healey, Defence Minister, visited Aden in June, 1965. Anthony Greenwood went in July and announced that a working party would meet in London to prepare for a constitutional conference later in the year: a halfway house to the earlier conference scheduled for March. The delegation duly arrived in London with Mackawee at its head. Now openly working with Abdullah al-Asnaj, who was not a member of the government party, Mackawee promptly demanded that the State of Emergency be lifted, all prisoners be released, and the future of the British base be placed on the agenda.

It was quite impossible for the British to accept these preliminary conditions without abandoning their plan, the execution of which was based on the assumption that, if they could steer it through the shoals of opposition and terrorism, it would work. It was realised that, in total freedom, Aden would never co-operate; but it was believed that, once imposed, most opponents would come to accept it. However, the British position was, by this time, almost impossible. Aden was pursuing a policy inside the Federation that the rulers would not accept; if Mackawee's terms were accepted the rulers would leave. The talks therefore dragged on uselessly to August 7 and then collapsed.

The British soldiered on. In September, they sent two experts, Sir Ralph Hone and Sir Gawain Bell, to prepare a draft constitution which they hoped would make the road to independence smoother. The High Commissioner amended the Public Service Regulations in October to enable more British posts in the administration to be filled by Arabs, and formed a new five-man committee to take over the commission's work. A month later, Lord Beswick, Parliamentary Under-Secretary for Commonwealth Relations and the Colonies, visited Aden to repeat that Britain hoped to establish a united independent republic, including Aden *and the Eastern Protectorate* by 1968. In seeking to emphasise in Aden that it was not the policy of the Labour government to support feudal chieftains, he came close to antagonising the federal rulers who constituted the only group of people on whom the High Commissioner could still rely. As a result, three federal ministers from the tribal area came to London in December to seek reassurance from Lord Longford, the new Colonial Secretary.

These efforts made no impact on the situation in Aden, which continued to deteriorate rapidly. In August 1965, Harry Barrie the British Superintendent of Police, and Sir Arthur Charles, Speaker of the State Legislative Assembly and former Speaker of the Aden Legislative Council, were both murdered. The death of the latter was a grim pointer to the fact that any Englishman was now the target of the terrorists, for Sir Arthur was a man respected and liked by the Adenis as a sympathetic and fair-minded man. A curfew was immediately imposed, and its hours had to be extended because terrorism continued unabated.

Order was crumbling, mainly because the security forces were working in an increasingly hostile atmosphere in which the public, either from fear or favour of the militant nationalists, would give them no help. The Aden government would not help the High Commission. When two members of the National Assembly proposed that Britain should negotiate with the NLF, they were supported in the debate by Abdel Qawee Mackawee. This was too much for the British government. On September 25, 1965, the High Commissioner suspended the Aden constitution and imposed direct rule because of the deteriorating security situation, the ministers' refusal to condemn terrorism and their support for the NLF—'the externally controlled instrument of terrorism'. The ministers were pleased to be released from their hazardous responsibilities.

II

As the situation in Aden worsened, Yemen seemed to be on the verge of peace. In August 1965, President Nasser met King Feisal* at Jeddah, where they reached agreement for an immediate cease-fire, the withdrawal of Egyptian troops by September 23, and an interim government to hold a plebiscite to determine the type of constitution for Yemen. This agreement set the stage for a peace conference of republicans and royalists to be held in the Yemeni village of Harad.

This sudden move by President Nasser was the outcome of eight months of political and military failure which began when the

---

*Prince Feisal had ascended the throne of Saudi Arabia in the previous autumn, when King Saud was deposed in his favour by the family and the religious leaders.

short-lived government of Hamud al-Gayefi was dismissed in January 1965 and Hassan al-Amri took office with a brief to crush the moderates. Amri formed a tribunal to try dissenting ministers, President Sallal broadcast that there would be no conciliation of royalists, and Nasser announced that the republic was 'here to stay'. The purpose of this hard line was to consolidate the political base for an offensive to crush all royalist opposition, to achieve which the number of Egyptian troops in Yemen had been raised to 70,000. It was launched against Harib, the town in the south across the border from Beihan, where 3,000 anti-Egyptian tribesmen had taken refuge. Harib was quickly captured but, before the month was out, the royalists recovered it with the support of these tribesmen. The Egyptian command was finding it more and more difficult to supply its forces in the north and south because the supply lines passed through unfriendly territory. Large numbers of its troops were permanently engaged in keeping the routes open; forward units were often cut off and had to be supplied by air. This happened in Harib, where the direct desert route from Sanaa was impossible and the alternative circuitous route took two weeks by convoy.

After this defeat, Nasser reversed his policy. He regrouped his forces on the central plateau where they could more easily take care of themselves, and sent for Ahmed Mohammed Noman to become Prime Minister. This was as striking a turn-about as the military withdrawal, for Noman was now leader of the republican 'third force' which wanted a negotiated peace. Its members were mainly the ministers against whom Amri had formed punitive tribunals, and its first leader, Sheikh Mohammed Zubeiri, had been murdered. It included Qadi Abdel Rahman Iryani, who had resigned from the Sallal government the preceding December; both he and Zubeiri had been vice-presidents under Sallal. The group's headquarters were in the village of Barat, a mountain stronghold near Saada, and it called itself the Party of Allah.

Noman formed his government on April 24, 1965, proclaiming his policy to be 'a return to peace in all parts of Yemen'. Although Sallal also stated that his government was determined to end the war, he was soon in conflict with Noman, and he appointed a

Supreme Council for the Armed Forces which became the effective government. When it ordered the arrest of a number of Noman's supporters on July 1, Noman resigned and flew to Cairo to protest to Nasser. Eighteen leading sheikhs and a number of moderate republicans, including Iryani, came to his support but their appeal was unsuccessful. Hassan al-Amri returned as Prime Minister, this time with a more flexible brief; and, after the Feisal-Nasser agreement in August, the republican factions were brought together in a Presidential Council which included Noman, Qadi Iryani and Hamud al-Gayefi. Noman's followers were released from prison.

The cease-fire was in effect, and the authoritative Cairo newspaper *Al-Ahram* stated on October 30 that Egyptian troops would be withdrawn at the rate of 10,000 a month for seven months *beginning* December 1—that is, more than two months after the date when the withdrawal should have been completed under the Jeddah agreement. This was one of the main reasons for the breakdown of the conference of royalists and republicans called in accordance with the Jeddah agreement. It opened on November 23, 1965 with twenty-five representatives of each side. Nasser and Feisal each sent one representative and a company of troops to guard the camp, erected at the little village of Harad in northern Yemen.

The aim of the conference was to elect an interim government which would hold a plebiscite, on the results of which it would frame a constitution and form a permanent government. But republicans insisted from the outset that the dynasty of the Imam's family must be excluded from all positions in the state. The royalists considered that this was a matter for the plebiscite, but in any case they were not willing to have a plebiscite while the Egyptian troops were in the country. Both sides made appeals to Nasser and Feisal; but, as neither was willing to make any concessions, the conference ground to a halt on the eve of the Muslim fast of Ramadan, December 24.

III

The withdrawal of the Egyptians at this point would have altered the situation in South Arabia in so far as it would have deprived the insurgent national forces of arms and ammunition, but it would not have made a decisive change. The resistance was indigenous enough to continue without Egyptian guidance from Taiz as long as enough weapons were left behind by Nasser's troops to sustain the fight. It was of importance, however, that the military parallels between the British and the Egyptian positions were now accentuated by the similarity of their political difficulties. The British could not come to terms with the extreme nationalists of Aden, and the Egyptians could not reconcile the moderate republicans to their policy. Neither could secure the body of support they needed.

The suspension of the constitution in Aden was a victory for the nationalists, who had made government impossible by any other means. The High Commissioner was committed to the suppression of terrorism and the Chief Minister to condoning it, so Britain was compelled to dismiss the government or abdicate. In choosing to impose direct rule, the British had, in effect, admitted their open confrontation with their extreme opponents, and there could be no turning back short of complete victory or complete defeat.

The opposition demands were unchanged: an end to the State of Emergency imposed in 1963, the withdrawal of the British military base, and free elections. The prospect of compromise was becoming more remote as the months passed and as moderate elements, from choice or fear of reprisals, went over to the extremists. The alliance of Abdullah al-Asnaj with the Labour government was over, and the PSP was beginning to rival the NLF in violence. Even the federal rulers issued a statement sympathetic to the demands of the Aden politicians, doubtless as a form of insurance against the victory of their enemies. They were now almost the only allies of the British, on whom their future entirely depended.

In mid-January 1966, the organisation of rebellion took a more definite form when OLOS joined forces with the NLF in a new organisation called the Front for the Liberation of South Yemen (thereafter known as FLOSY), which received the blessing both of the Arab League and Yemen. It was an uneasy partnership from the outset and not one that would last, but at the time it reflected the hardening of opinion against the British policy and, in particular, the acceptance of violence as a method by Asnaj's PSP. Abdel Qawee Mackawee, who had called on the High Commissioner to recognise the NLF as a negotiating body, helped to bring Asnaj and Qahtan as-Shaabi together and became secretary-general of FLOSY. Its first act was to set up a revolutionary headquarters in Taiz, from which the NLF was already operating, to direct armed struggle inside the Federation.

The High Commissioner sought to win over the South Arabian League, which had opposed the formation of FLOSY, by giving its exiled leaders permission to return to Aden, but it was more than their lives were worth to accept this belated gesture. To make sure that his nationalism was not called in question, Mohammed Ali Jifri proclaimed that the future of South Arabia should be 'determined in confrontation with Britain'. The federal ministers also tried to break the cohesion of the nationalist front by arranging meetings with its constituent groups in Beirut. They managed to get two representatives from FLOSY to attend the first in April, but both were promptly disowned by their party, and by the time the third and last meeting took place in October, even the SAL refused to make any agreement.

As the opposition became more and more formidable, the cost to Britain continued to rise. In 1964–65, it gave the Federation aid to the value of £14·2 million, and in January 1966 announced a development loan—which was bound to be a gift—of £4·2 million, most of which was intended to improve conditions in the tribal area in an effort to bring it a little nearer to the standards of Aden. This had been inevitable ever since the formation of the Federation, but it appeared as though Britain was trying to buy goodwill for the federal scheme. Before 1956, the Protectorate states had received only £523,000 in grants, and in 1955–60 only £770,000; whereas, in the same five-year period, Aden had received £7·2 million for development, most of which had gone to the vital improvement of the port. Whatever contributions Britain now gave to the Federation were considered to be too little—and too late.

8

Britain's Volte Face

T HE MILITANT resistance movement was fighting under very changed circumstances in 1966, for in Britain there had been a dramatic change in defence planning that had profound effects on South Arabia. On February 22, a new Defence White Paper was issued which declared that all British troops would be withdrawn from Aden by December 31, 1968, and that there would be no defence treaty with the South Arabian Federation after independence. The whole intention of British policy up to that moment had been to retain the base almost at any cost. The reversal of this policy, as part of the recasting of British defence commitments East of Suez, made it certain that there could not be an orderly settlement of the problem of South Arabia.

I

It was manifestly impossible to withdraw a vital element of the plan and hope that the rest of it would hold together. The tribal rulers and moderate Adenis had trusted themselves to the Federation in the absolute, and justifiable, confidence that they would be protected against internal and external enemies for a long time to come. They had always assumed that they would continue to have a large part of the money accruing to them from the British troops, which amounted to £11 million a year and was a quarter of Aden's annual income. Every British statement had confirmed this belief; indeed, the impression given to the Adenis was that the base would be

148

retained whether the Arabs wanted it or not, and for that reason it was the primary object of nationalist criticism.

The British decision to leave Aden in 1968 intensified the struggle for power among the Adenis and tribal rulers, and made it certain that they would fight among themselves. Who would rule South Arabia would not be determined by negotiation and planning but by a knock-out fight which would determine who was strongest. On the face of it, the Adenis should have been displeased and the federal rulers pleased, because the army was a tribal affair and could therefore impose the will of the tribes on the town: a prospect that had frightened the people of Aden from the outset. Yet the opposite was true. The rulers were shocked and the militant nationalists pleased because there was a large and well-equipped Egyptian army across the borders in Yemen which could, they believed, be relied on to come at the first call to defend nationalists against the 'imperialist stooges' of the hinterland. The fears of the rulers and the hopes of the militants seemed immediately justified when Nasser broke the Jeddah agreement with Feisal by announcing that he would also keep his troops in Yemen until the end of 1968. 'The Ministers of the federal government complain bitterly that Britain is leaving them at the mercy of Egyptian aggression and Russian penetration', reported David Holden from Aden in March 1967.*

For shopkeepers, taxi-drivers and officials in government and private business, the British decision was viewed as a calamity. They had not wanted either the merger or independence in the first place, but had consoled themselves with the hope that the British would be around long enough to ensure that the new state got firmly on its feet. Their fears had risen as terrorism increased, and now they foresaw nothing but trouble and a real danger of chaos after the British left. Above all, the Indian traders realised that in two years they would be at the mercy of Arabs who did not want them in Aden.

The security position was greatly weakened because there was clearly no future in helping the British. For this reason, the federal ministers had tried to come to terms with the militants in Beirut,

Sunday Times, March 12, 1967.

and they now began to make statements more in keeping with militant sentiment. The High Commissioner found it impossible to fill the twenty-four places allotted to Aden in the Federal Council because FLOSY had threatened to murder any Adeni joining it. When, in spite of this, six men agreed to become members in February, one of them immediately withdrew after angry demonstrations outside his house.* No member of the public was willing to give any help or information to the security officers, whether British or Arab, and even the police were unwilling to see or hear anything that might put them in the position of informing against either FLOSY or NLF members.

The militants attacked with greater frequency and almost with impunity. British troops could do little to prevent them because they were debarred from taking preventive action. Even before the decision to withdraw the base, terrorism had risen to fearful proportions: one incident in 1963, 36 incidents in 1964, 286 in 1965, and almost double this last figure in 1966. The security authorities rounded up fifty-five suspected terrorists in Sheikh Othman and the Mansoura suburb of Aden on March 22 after two murders in broad daylight. The assassin in each case was allowed to escape. Six people were murdered in the last two weeks of March, one of the victims being a woman tourist who had come off a boat to do some shopping.

The federal ministers still hoped that, in the end, they would get some promise of support by the British government. In the meanwhile, however, they announced publicly that they would not ask for a defence treaty but would seek from Britain heavy guns, armoured cars, an air force and training facilities. They were making the best of a bad job because Lord Beswick had already categorically refused their request for a ten-year defence agreement. In May 1966, a group of ministers came to London to present their requirements, and the British government undertook to give £5½ million for the expansion of the federal army and to increase its annual contribution

---

*One of them, Abdel Rahman Basendwah, was murdered on August 19, but the remaining four agreed to become ministers. The Federal Council met for the first time in over a year on August 6, 1966.

to the running costs by £2½ million. British contributions before this offer were £5 million as a general subsidy to the Federation and £4·6 million for equipping and training the army. The cost of running the army was more than the total income of the federal government, so that it was clear that, unless the British paid for it, there would be no security forces at all after the evacuation of the base.

The situation was worsening rapidly because the NLF broke away from FLOSY in December 1966 and formed its own fifteen-man executive under Qahtan as-Shaabi, the membership of which was otherwise secret. In immediate response to this, FLOSY formed, under Mohammed al-Magaali, its own militant wing of nine units, all of which were equipped by Egyptian Intelligence. As FLOSY had only lately come into the terrorist campaign, Asnaj and Mackawee had very little contact with or control over it. This new organisation was named the Popular Organisation of Revolutionary Forces (PORF), and its task was not only to compete with the NLF in patriotic violence but also to ensure that, if terror was to be used by Arab against Arab (as well as against the 'collaborators'), FLOSY would not be at the mercy of its dangerous rival.

The formation of PORF was encouraged by Egypt and marked the beginning of Egyptian support for FLOSY against the NLF. The impetuous Qahtan as-Shaabi—a difficult man to handle at any time—was disinclined to accept Egyptian orders, and the government in Cairo came to the conclusion that he would prove an impossible ally if at any time he ceased to have his more cautious cousin, Feisal as-Shaabi, at his elbow. By comparison, the political sophistication of Abdullah al-Asnaj made him seem easy company. The effect of this policy was eventually to do harm to FLOSY and to improve the position of the NLF in South Arabia, where the people as a whole, though prepared to accept Egyptian money and arms, were not willing to be subservient.

Asnaj and Mackawee were energetically pursuing a claim to precedence in the resistance movement by every propaganda means available. In April 1966, Mackawee had told a press conference in Damascus that FLOSY would continue the armed struggle in South

Arabia 'until complete victory has been achieved with the evacuation of the British imperialists from the country'. He declared that the Front was resolutely acting to expand the armed battle so that it could include the remaining areas in South Arabia, adding that the Front assumed 'the responsibility of the armed struggle in the South, in addition to the Aden front where the commandos are waging the noblest and most valiant battles against the forces of the British occupation'.* Coming from a man whose militancy was of recent date, this was gall to Qahtan as-Shaabi. The NLF was part of FLOSY at that time, but if the group of Mackawee and Asnaj succeeded in assuming the leadership of the resistance movement, the probability was that it alone would inherit power when the British left. Mackawee's statements therefore provoked the withdrawal of the NLF from FLOSY and made inevitable an eventual conflict between the two movements.

The South Arabian League had by this time drifted into a position not very much different from that of the rulers, for it had little chance of power except through the British. The Jifri brothers had not returned to Aden, but the secretary of the SAL, Sheikhan al-Habshi, went back there and made some obscure and indirect contacts with the High Commission. The League was now receiving financial support from Saudi Arabia (which was an additional reason for Egypt's hostility to it), and it seemed likely that, if it came to a fight for power after the British left, it would be driven to the side of the rulers and Saudi Arabia against the militants and their Egyptian supporters.

Less than three weeks after the announcement that the base at Aden was to be abandoned, and in the absence of a defence commitment by Britain, proposals for the constitution of the new state were published. Known as the Hone-Bell proposals from the names of the two civil servants who prepared them, this draft constitution was mooted at the very time when the battle lines were being drawn and when it was already apparent that the opportunity for a constructive political initiative by Britain had vanished. The Hone-Bell proposals were circulated by the federal government to all Arab states, to the

Mideast Mirror, February 12, 1966.

Arab League Secretariat and to the United Nations. Sultan Saleh bin Hussein al-Audhali, at that time chairman of the Supreme Council, announced that the draft would be circulated throughout South Arabia for study and 'amendment according to the will of the people'.*

The draft constitution provided for a National Assembly formed by direct election, or by indirect election where necessary in tribal areas; a Council of States with the right to review, but not veto, legislation of the Assembly; a Prime Minister responsible to the Assembly, and a President with limited constitutional powers. It proposed that Aden should become the capital of the new state (which, to all intents and purposes, it was bound to be, whatever ministries were tucked away in Al-Ittihad), that there should be a Minister for Aden Affairs, and that Adenis should make up one-third of the Council of States. The Hone-Bell constitution was immediately condemned by Mackawee as a new British plot to impose a false constitution on the people of 'the occupied South'; and most Adenis considered that, despite the concessions to Aden, it was still weighted in favour of the tribal rulers. Judged objectively, it was an excellent and fair attempt to produce a constitution for a difficult region, but it suffered from the major defect that it had no hope of acceptance. As *The Economist* pointed out, 'any constitutional plan devised by two British officials hired by the federal sheikhs—who are themselves regarded as "stooges of the British"—was bound to be shot down in flames without ever getting off the ground'.†

The federal ministers and the British were gradually giving ground. A resolution of the United Nations General Assembly in November 1965 had called for elections by universal suffrage under UN supervision, the lifting of the State of Emergency, the release of prisoners and the abandonment of the British base. This had not been accepted, either by the British, who at that time were still intent on keeping the base, or by the federal ministers, who desired a British presence of some sort. In certain respects, such as

*Mideast Mirror, February 12, 1966.

†*The Economist*, February 26, 1966.

the conditions governing elections, the constitution issued by the federal government was a rejection of the resolution. The militant opposition, of course, made acceptance of the resolution, particularly its call for elections by universal suffrage, a primary demand. On May 13, 1966, however, the federal government publicly accepted the resolution. Both FLOSY and the federal government sent missions to the autumn session of the United Nations, and there Lord Caradon confirmed the British acceptance of the resolution of November 1965. He then went further, reversing British objection to UN participation of the state-making process by asking for a UN mission to facilitate South Arabia's advance to independence. This was a clear recognition by Britain that its efforts to bring the federal government and the opposition into negotiations for a settlement had failed.

The final twist was yet to come. Mackawee had already condemned the federal government's acceptance of the UN resolution as 'a farce and a mockery'. When the United Nations Trusteeship Committee agreed in principle on December 2, 1966, to send a mission, he declared FLOSY's opposition to this and warned of the dangers the mission would face if it went to Aden. This, in effect, was an admission by Mackawee and his associates of their realisation that no fair-minded mission would impose FLOSY as the sole representative of the South Arabian people and establish its power —which was the Front's aim.

The errors committed by the British were now being compounded by the total intransigence of the militants. If their true objective was simply a free and independent state under conditions that would ensure fair elections and establish the will of the people, this they now had within their power to achieve. The British had undertaken to grant independence, had promised to withdraw their base, had agreed that the United Nations should supervise elections and had asked for a mission to facilitate the interim measures. Even the ill-fated Hone-Bell constitution was only a draft which they had been asked to amend. Every death and wound of the coming bloody year, and the progressive ruin caused to the economy, were unnecessary.

II

The fighting on the frontier with Yemen was by this time being instigated by the NLF and FLOSY, except for a Yemeni air raid on a village in Beihan in July 1966. Colonel J. W. G. Gray, commander of the Hadraumi Bedouin Legion was murdered on July 28, and Abdullah al-Asnaj broadcast his approval of the deed from Radio Cairo.

In republican Yemen, the situation was far from happy because of the conflict within the political camp. The ill-health of Sallal enabled the Egyptian government to keep him out of the way in Cairo while the Prime Minister, Hassan al-Amri sought to reconcile Egyptian policy with that of the 'third force' leaders by arguing that, while evacuation of Egyptian troops and agreement with the royalists was the aim, it could only be achieved from a strong position. President Sallal returned to Sanaa in August 1966, obviously with a brief to try his strong-arm policy again. Almost at once he came into conflict with Amri, who was not a man of dove-like outlook. The position of Sallal was by no means secure. Egyptian tanks guarded his house, the airport and all important buildings in the city.

The rumour soon grew that Amri was under house-arrest preparatory to being removed to Cairo on the grounds, it was said, that he had turned against the Egyptians and was plotting with the 'third force' to protest to the United Nations against the 'occupation'. What may have been a premature rumour became a hard fact. In most obscure circumstances, Amri was arrested with about forty of his supporters, including Qadi Abdel Rahman al-Iryani, Ahmed Mohammed Noman and nine members of his cabinet, all of whom found themselves in detention in Cairo. According to the 'third force' people, they were on their way to New York but were seized at the airport and put on a plane for Cairo.

Sallal formed a new government in September 1966 with himself as Prime Minister as well as President, and brought in General Abdullah Guzeilan as deputy prime minister and deputy commander-in-chief, thereby making him second to himself both in civil and military affairs. No one of importance in the republican revolution was now with Sallal; if they were not in Cairo they were touring the Arab world to protest to its governments against the continuing Egyptian occupation. It was a Yemeni version of direct rule in Aden, for Nasser could only hold his position in Yemen by imposing his authority; but there was a vital difference in that the Yemeni opposition had no promise of better times to come.

One of the first acts of the new Sallal government was to form a Committee of Inquiry to investigate the activities of people 'working against the interests of the state'. In October 1966, seven opponents of the régime were tried, found guilty and executed all in one day. There were so many arrests that schools, government offices and army barracks were converted into prisons. Mohammed Ahmed Noman, son of Ahmed Mohammed, the former Prime Minister detained in Cairo, described these acts as 'the liquidation of the pillars of the revolution', and the International Commission of Jurists in Geneva cabled Sallal that, in view of the speed of the arrests, trials and executions, they deemed it impossible that justice could have been done. Undeterred, Sallal continued the purges. On December 3, five men were shot in front of a crowd of 4,000 only fifteen minutes after the verdict, and their bodies were hung on the gates of the city. Two others suffered the same fate on December 5.

The civil war had taken a similarly unpleasant turn following the failure to reconvene the abortive Harad conference and of an attempt at arbitration by the Sultan of Kuwait. President Nasser announced in March 1966 his new policy of 'the long breath'. He would, he said, abandon positions of no importance and stay in Yemen for twenty years if necessary to ensure that the republican army could safeguard the revolution. There was still, in theory, a cease-fire in operation, but there were frequent reports of infringements. The consolidation of the Egyptian army on the plateau enabled the royalists virtually to take over two-thirds of the country in circumstances that led to the defection of pro-republican tribes to them. The Egyptian command, no longer hazarding ground troops where it was not absolutely necessary, and finding that high-explosive bombs had little effect in the mountains, resorted to the use of napalm and poison gas.*

King Feisal was meanwhile standing by his demand for the withdrawal of Egyptian troops and the formation of an interim government consisting of an equal number of royalists and republicans; but he was still keeping the royalists supplied with arms and money. He was angry with the British because of their decision to withdraw from Aden without offering a defence agreement, firmly believing that Nasser would not evacuate Yemen now that he saw the chance of helping the pro-Egyptian parties to power in South Arabia without any risk of clashing with British troops. Feisal was also convinced that Russia had encouraged Nasser to break the Jeddah agreement and was now doing its utmost to establish a position, or at least allies, on the Red Sea littoral of the Arabian peninsula. In his view, the security of his own state was greatly weakened as a result of Britain's mismanagement of South Arabia and failure to guarantee its safety.

III

It was not until December 13, 1966 that the United Nations General Assembly confirmed the Trusteeship Committee's decision to send a three-man mission to 'facilitate' South Arabian independence, and another month went by before U Thant found a chairman for it. By this time, the sands were running out very fast. There had been 531 incidents in 1966 and the death rate was rising steadily. British troops could at best slow down the rate of blood-letting as they struggled to keep something like order in a sea of uncoöperative, unfriendly or downright murderous people.

'During the past month, this lawlessness has reached appalling proportions with the whole life of our port brought to a standstill

*Reports of the use of poison gas first appeared in the *Daily Telegraph* and then came from other sources. Wilfred Thesiger, the well-known Arabian traveller, reported its use in press interviews and then in *The Times*, but it remained in doubt for lack of scientific evidence until the summer of 1966, when the Red Cross at last confirmed it.

and with unequalled scenes of brutality', wrote Hussein Ali Bayoomi in a letter to *The Times* in March 1967, referring to the violence of the national struggle. He went on:

> I wonder, Sir, whether your readers can imagine what it is like to live under these terrible conditions. Do they really think that we Adenis, who are a trading nation proud of our port and our commerce, would wilfully plunge our state into bloodshed and destruction? Can they imagine an existence where no man dares to speak out against this Egyptian threat to our freedom for fear of almost certain death at the hands of an assassin? Can they imagine whole families ordered out into the streets by paid Yemeni terrorists to take part in demonstrations which they loathe and deplore?*

This picture of the situation was not exaggerated and it was also true that Yemenis and tribesmen from the former Protectorate states were mainly responsible for the outrages. Many Adenis deplored the violence and the parties provoking it, holding Egypt responsible for a great deal of it. The fact remained that they were afraid to oppose it; and as time passed, and the British troops could neither protect them nor stop the violence, they too began to blame the troops and to wish they would be gone. They had reached the rock-bottom position where they were willing to accept anything that brought peace to Aden.

Duncan Sandys, the former Colonial Secretary, who had done so much towards the manufacture of the Federation and the Aden merger, wrote to *The Times* on March 3 that 'the responsibility for law and order should be transferred as soon as practicable to the federal government'. This view rested on the assumption that the government was composed of fine, brave fellows who were willing to fight for themselves, but, if they had ever been so, they were no longer in the mood for courage after they learnt that the British troops were going to leave them. The strong-willed Sharif of

*The Times, March 11, 1967. Bayoomi wrote as secretary-general of the United National Party of Aden, the party of his late brother Hassan, but he was also one of the Adeni ministers in the federal government.

Beihan, who had been the strongest advocate of the Federation back in the fifties, was its natural leader, and as Minister of Interior should have been attending to security. But he had pulled out of Al-Ittihad two years earlier and engaged himself in the more practical work of strengthening his contacts with Yemeni royalists and Saudis over his northern border. The government was a leaderless group with a small, anxious administration keeping things going as best it could.

The one hope left for controlling the situation seemed to be the South Arabian Army with its British commander and officers. At the beginning of March 1967, it was agreed that one battalion would take over security operations in Crater, doubtless with a view to extending its control to other parts of Aden as the British withdrew. The experiment, in fact, failed; but most British people in Aden had by this time come round to the view that it was essential to rebuild security through the Arabian force well before the withdrawal of British troops. The British civil and military authorities, however, had serious misgiving about the federal army. There was still the fear, generated by the Adenis themselves, that its tribesmen would be cruel and vengeful towards townsmen. There was also the possibility that the propaganda of the militants might have affected the officers more deeply than was apparent, making them more of a security risk than a help. Nor could anyone be certain that there were not supporters of FLOSY and the NLF among them who would split the army apart when put in charge of civilian security.

The High Commission was still pinning its faith on the federal government and the army for lack of anywhere else to turn, but with deepening pessimism. Of the Adeni ministers, two were still working hard, even behaving as though an effective government still existed. They were Abdul Rahman Girgerah, the Minister of National Guidance and Information, and Hussein Ali Bayoomi, the Minister of Civil Aviation. Bayoomi had courageously threatened to deport 48,000 Yemenis if they supported a strike called by FLOSY in February; FLOSY replied over Radio Cairo that it had passed sentence of death on him, and the strike took place. Bayoomi left for the United Nations to present the federal case.

The government in London was approaching the conclusion that its South Arabian policy was at a dead-end. The hope that the United Nations mission might get it off the hook was fading fast as conflicts within the camp of the militants made any chance of a consensus of national opinion more remote every day.

9

The End of an Affair

AT THE END of February 1967, Sheikh Mohammed Farid, the
federal Foreign Minister and one of the best of the tribal leaders in
the Supreme Council, accompanied by Girgerah, went to London
to warn the British government that it was impossible to discuss a
date for independence unless there were some cast-iron guarantees
of protection for the new state. They were allowed to air this demand
for a reversal of British policy for a fortnight, but were promised
nothing.

They were successful, however, in compelling the British to make
up their minds whether they were going to put all their eggs in the
federal basket. As this was too difficult a decision to make in London,
on March 17 George Thomson, Minister of State at the Foreign
Office, was despatched to Aden to sound out reactions to a plan to
grant independence to South Arabia in November. Although he
promised that the British government would provide air cover for
the new state after independence, he did not give assurance of any
other military support, and his proposal shocked the federal government. The High Commissioner, Sir Richard Turnbull, told him
that there was every possibility that the federal army would use
violently repressive measures when the British left, and therefore
Britain should not remain in the picture once the federal government took over.

On his return from Aden two days later Thomson informed the
press that it was Britain's duty and right to decide the best date for
independence. Nevertheless, George Brown, the Foreign Secretary,

did not announce November as the date of independence—as was expected—when he addressed the House of Commons on March 20. It was clear that he still hoped that the belated United Nations Mission would be able to broaden the base of discussions and help to produce a peaceful advance to independence. To that end, the British were willing to allow all the militants in exile to return to Aden for discussions with the mission. The Foreign Secretary told the House that, in correspondence with President Nasser, he had pointed out that terrorism in Aden was wrong and senseless, but had received no assurance that Nasser would do anything to stop it.

I

The UN mission had by this time been chosen. It consisted of Dr Manuel Pérez-Guerrero, head of the Venezuelan delegation, an intellectual and linguist who knew Arabic and was acquainted with Nasser, Abdel Sattar Shelizi, former deputy prime minister of Afghanistan, and Moussa Leo Keita of Mali, who was described by the *Observer* as 'a gentle, studious man' but was anti-British and strongly left-wing. The choice of Keita was disliked by the federal ministers, who could see him supporting the Aden militants all the way. The mission was set to its task in terms which contradicted themselves, for, although the Assembly was unanimous that the members should not go to Aden with preconditions for independence, at the same time it endorsed recommendations of the Committee on Colonialism which were totally anti-British and anti-federal.

The prospects for success were practically extinguished before the mission arrived in Cairo on its way to Aden, for the Egyptian government had concluded already that no plebiscite was now necessary in Aden as FLOSY was acknowledged by the people of South Arabia to be their sole representative. The leaders of FLOSY refused to meet the mission (although there was a hint they might do so if it went to their headquarters in Taiz in Yemen), and the NLF demanded prior conditions which totally prejudged the issue: the lifting of the State of Emergency, the release of political prisoners and an undertaking by the mission that it would refuse to meet anyone concerned with the federal government. A general strike in Aden was called by FLOSY, which also gave instructions to increase terrorism during the mission's visit.

On arrival in Aden on April 2, 1967, the UN mission was put in the Seaview Hotel, which was heavily guarded. Its members had a formal meeting with the High Commissioner and his staff on the following morning at which they refused to deal with the federal government except through him. After this meeting (which was to be their only formal consultation with the High Commissioner), the members of the mission vanished into their hotel for two days, during which they were not seen at all.

The circumstances were adverse. The general strike was in full swing and there were no less than seventy incidents on the first day of the visit. Then Aden had one of its rare rainstorms; this had the advantage of stopping violence but it brought life in Aden to a halt, cut the telephone system, and kept British troops active cleaning out the town. The mission then emerged on April 5 to go to Mansoura prison where the political detainees were held, only to be abused by rival factions of NLF and FLOSY prisoners who, on the instructions of their leaders, would not talk to the UN representatives. During the visit to the prison noisy bazookas and automatic weapons kept up a staged battle-din outside, and the mission was finally taken over the top of it by helicopter to regain its hotel.

At their meeting on April 3, the UN representatives had asked the High Commissioner to arrange for them to broadcast on television to the people of South Arabia, and he persuaded the federal ministers, whom the mission would not recognise as the government but whose station it was, to agree to this. When the text of the broadcast was seen by Hussein Ali Bayoomi on April 6, he discovered it was anti-federal and specifically stated that the mission would not recognise the government. The federal ministers hastily consulted together and banned the broadcast. At this, the members of the mission blamed the British and announced their immediate departure; and although by next morning when they left they had received a telegram from U Thant telling them to stay, they went on their way. It was the end of the expedition. They remained in Geneva for a while, but their cogitations brought no positive action and they returned to New York. Although neither the Egyptians nor the militant movements had talked to them, and had positively hindered their work by the strike and violence, the UN representatives still accused Britain of sabotaging their work.

The mission's visit to Aden made a bad situation worse. On February 28, a bomb planted by the house servant exploded during a British dinner party at a flat in Maala, killing two women and wounding others. Sir Richard Turnbull advised soldiers not to bring their children out for the Easter holidays; but the army, reckoning that they could look after them, let them come, despite FLOSY statements that, though they would not attack women and children, they could not help it if they got in the way of grenades. Crater was becoming less and less safe as days went by.*

The three-sided Arab war, between PORF and the NLF and between them both and the supporters of the federal government, continued bitterly. In February 1967, three of Mackawee's four sons were killed by a time-bomb placed on the window-sill of his house. This may have been intended only as a warning to Mackawee, who was in Yemen, and the deaths accidental, but in mid-April a time-bomb was found just after take-off by the pilot of a plane in which he was flying to Yemen. Between March 16 and April 14, there was a murder a day as trade unionists of the rival movements pursued their vendetta. Salem al-Amoudi, the father-in-law of Mohammed Salem Basendwah of FLOSY, was shot five times in Sheikh Othman and died in hospital. Abdel Rahim Kasim, a member of the Aden government from 1963 to 1965 and a supporter of Mackawee, was murdered as he stepped inside his car after visiting the dying Amoudi. As this war went on, it appeared that the NLF

---

*I stayed for the last time at the Besse Guest House in Crater in May 1967, and already by then one sometimes ate to the sound of small-arms fire outside the house. The experienced Reuter correspondent, Ibrahim Noori, circumnavigated a gun battle at the main crossroads to get me to an appointment at the High Commission. Some businessmen continued to use Crater afterwards, but it was hazardous until the British troops finally took charge of the town.

was having the best of it, and the British now realised for the first time the extent of its organisation. Sheikh Othman, Crater and Maala were covered with huge *graffiti* clearly revealing which areas were held by NLF and which by FLOSY. Yet FLOSY, which was not proscribed because it was a political party (whereas the NLF was proscribed because it was considered to be 'a gang of thugs'), continued to identify its men in Aden by regularly holding parades, usually in the form of processions at the funerals of its fallen.

II

The abortive UN mission left a great deal of ill-will between the High Commission and the federal government when it departed. The ministers were annoyed because the Commission blamed them for the break-down over the broadcast, and more than annoyed by its attempt to stop them publishing their version of events afterwards. This did not help in London, where the government already felt that one more chance of finding a peaceful settlement had vanished with the failure of the mission.

Although Sir Richard Turnbull had uneasy relations with the federal ministers, it remained his view that the only solution available, if the UN could not bring all the various elements together, was for Britain to bolster the federal government and see that it was secure. This was the policy being advocated by the Conservative opposition with considerable strength, but it did not appeal to Harold Wilson's cabinet, whose members believed that so narrow a government would not bring peace to South Arabia. In this they were right, but Sir Richard was also right in his belief that it was impossible to bring the NLF and FLOSY into any sort of collaboration.

In this quandary, George Brown decided to despatch another emissary, this time Lord Shackleton, Minister without Portfolio, with an open brief to see what new ideas could come forward. Lord Shackleton took with him an experienced and able Arabist, Samuel Falle, who was called in haste from Malaysia for the job. They arrived in Aden on April 12 and immediately began to take a fresh look at the situation by talking to everyone they could contact,

G

from friendly moderates and federal ministers to any less open contacts that Falle could make. They threw their nets wider, seeking conversations—secret if necessary—with the rival militants. At one stage it seemed that they might meet Abdullah al-Asnaj in Geneva, but Asnaj backed down at the last minute.

Lord Shackleton came to one very clear conclusion: that distinguished as Sir Richard Turnbull had been throughout his career, he was not the best man for this particular job. The full recommendations were not published but it seems clear that they urged that a last, final, sustained and radical effort should be made under a new man to bring all the elements, including the militants, into discussions about independence and the road to it. Lord Shackleton recommended that Sir Humphrey Trevelyan, who had lately retired from the Foreign Office on completion of his assignment as ambassador to the USSR, should come back into harness for this most difficult task. Sir Humphrey was persuaded to do so and he arrived in Aden in the early hours of May 21. That morning he called the press to the High Commission to receive a statement:

The creation of a new independent country is a task which must surely have universal approval. I have great sympathy for the people of South Arabia and am very glad to have the opportunity to help them to independence. Under the guidance of the Foreign Secretary I am here to take up the task of my distinguished predecessor, Sir Richard Turnbull, for whom I have great respect and who did much to help this country forward, in the face of many difficulties; since, as the Foreign Secretary said in the House of Commons on 11 May, he considers that the problem has moved into a new phase in which the kind of experience I have had will be of help. In the same statement the Foreign Secretary made it clear that our purpose is to withdraw our military forces, as we have undertaken to do, and to bring into being an independent state with a stable and secure government.

My first task will be to study the situation on the spot. The problems of South Arabia are complicated but our approach to them is simple. In our consideration of these problems, we start from a position of support for the Federal Government which is the legal government of South Arabia and with which we shall work in close co-operation. It has already done much to build up the South Arabian state. We agree with the Federal Government's view that they and political leaders not represented in their ranks should be united in the common task. I am for my part ready to talk to representatives of any South Arabian party who are ready to talk with me with a view to that end; and we look for United Nations help in arranging discussions between the parties. The United Nations resolution, which we have accepted, provides the general framework for the future. What we should like to achieve is a central caretaker government, broad-based and representing the whole of South Arabia. The United Nations have called for such a government, which the Federal Government and all others of goodwill would like to see formed and which can only come into being with the agreement of all parties concerned. I hope for the co-operation of all political groups in constructive efforts to achieve this end and so bring South Arabia to independence under most favourable conditions. But, whether we are completely successful in this or not, our central task is to ensure that South Arabia will come to independence under the best conditions possible and will be able to defend that independence and develop the economy for the benefit of the people.

It is clearly necessary that that violence should stop. It is intolerable that all efforts of both governments and the United Nations to make progress towards independence and ensure the security of life and property should be threatened by a handful of people acting in a way which is totally opposed to the true interests of South Arabia. I should like to make it quite clear that I intend to maintain law and order. For this purpose security measures are necessary and can be combined with political measures at the right time, if there are indications that they will have favourable effect. We shall therefore continue to combat violence while at the same time trying to make all political leaders understand that it is against their interests and the interests of the country and that the right way of resolving political differences is by calm political discussion.

This was the policy pursued by Britain to the end. In effect, it said that the federal government was all the British had at the moment and they would support it accordingly unless and until they could broaden it by securing the support of other political groups; and, in the meanwhile, everything would be done to keep the peace inside the country. The onus rested with the NLF and FLOSY; if they did not want the existing federal government, they should come along and help to change it by agreement. The call to them was clear and unambiguous. Sir Humphrey summoned a meeting of his security chiefs the moment the press had left his room at the residence.

Military action showed greater firmness, but it could do little to stop the violence which lurked in every back street of Aden's labyrinthine Arab quarters and invaded the main streets whenever possible. The six-day Arab-Israeli war in early June 1967 and the devastating defeat of the Arabs did not improve the situation because of the false accusation that Britain had supported Israel, but the situation was already so bad that it was not notably changed by it. Sir Humphrey, nevertheless, continued in communication with Lord Shackleton to prepare detailed plans for the implementation of the policy that a reluctant British government would need to accept if there was to be any chance of success.

This detailed plan was presented to the House of Commons by the Foreign Secretary, George Brown, on June 20 and went some way to meet the federal government's demands for more security. It provided for about £10 million more in money, self-loading rifles, armoured cars and field artillery for the army and a military mission after independence to help with advice and training. Provision was made for supplying and financing the operation of eight Hunter aircraft in addition to the Jet Provost ground-attack aircraft which had already been promised. As it was considered that the internal security problem might be aggravated after independence by intervention from outside (which clearly implied by Egyptian intervention through Yemen), Britain undertook to station a naval force in South Arabian waters for six months after independence, from which aircraft could strike against any aggressor. V-bombers would also be stationed at Masirah Island, off the Arabian coast, for the first six months, and longer if it were deemed necessary.

The Foreign Secretary said he had reluctantly approved the recommendation of Sir Humphrey and Lord Shackleton that trial by jury should be suspended as long as Britain was still there; he had been convinced that the failure to get convictions of terrorists because witnesses were intimidated was a serious obstacle to public safety. On the other hand, he accepted their recommendation that the proscription of the NLF should be lifted because it did not inhibit terrorism but was a bar to useful negotiations. He announced that independence would be granted to South Arabia on January 9, 1968, after the Ramadan fast, and that British troops would complete their withdrawal. Meanwhile, the British Government accepted in respect of Aden state (i.e. the Colony, which was still its responsibility) the Hone-Bell constitution as amended and circulated by the South Arabian government, in which there was now provision for the formation of a more broadly based caretaker government immediately this was possible. Britain would accept this constitution for the whole of South Arabia immediately if transitional arrangements were made.

The door was wide open. It only remained for FLOSY and the NLF to come forward, help to construct the broadly based government, accept the financial assistance offered, and reject British proposals for external defence if they did not want it.

III

On the day that the Foreign Secretary was offering the Federation a chance to reach independence in an orderly way, the first crack in the federal front occurred. The army mutinied. This had nothing to do with the political situation but revealed how tribal passions were still powerful underneath the veneer of discipline.

Four colonels believed that they had been unfairly treated because of tribal preference in promotions and sent a petition to the federal Minister of Defence, who suspended them on June 16. This act angered their own tribesmen in the ranks. They seized arms from the armoury and with machine guns mowed down eight men of the British Royal Corps of Transport as they were driving away from routine practice at a range opposite Champion Lines where the mutiny started. At the request of the federal government, who saw the mutiny spreading without restraint, British troops moved in to halt it. This they did at a cost to themselves of seventeen dead and twenty-two wounded.

News of this clash, interpreted by rumour as a revolt of the federal army against the British, spread to Crater, where police recruits stampeded to seize weapons. The armed police then took to their arms and in a series of encounters several British troops were killed there also. The belief that the army was in revolt against the British had brought to the surface the militant allegiances of the internal security force, and the British troops evacuated Crater while the High Commission and the British military commanders measured the meaning of it all.

The suspicion in the minds of the British authorities that the federal ministers would prove broken reeds in the end stood confirmed by their complete collapse in the face of the emergency. Although the mutiny had not been caused by the political movements, it had provoked FLOSY and NLF adherents, to whom it was immediately apparent that there was nothing to fear from the federal government. Crater had demonstrated that there was no internal security force worth speaking of.

For a fortnight, Crater was in the hands of the nationalists. Then the Argyll and Sutherland Highlanders moved in swiftly, and they fiercely restored order. Their methods resulted in a petition from 700 Adeni Arabs who accused them of brutality. To this John Wilton, the Deputy High Commissioner, replied by pointing to the murder and kidnapping of innocent and guilty alike during the Arab control of the district, which could only be stopped by firm action. The soldiers' riposte to any attack on them was so sharp and vigorous that the militants' losses were much greater than their own. The Scots were feared in Crater, but they maintained a brooding peace until they finally withdrew in November 1967.

The events of June 20 convinced the High Commissioner that the federal government must be changed. He put pressure on the

Supreme Council until it agreed to let Hussein Ali Bayoomi try to form a broadly based caretaker government with himself as premier-designate, and to undertake to step down once the government was formed. Bayoomi succeeded, after considerable difficulty, in getting seven people to agree to join a ministry. Sir Humphrey thereupon left for New York on the next stage of his plan: to persuade the UN mission to resume its good offices in South Arabia.

In the High Commissioner's absence, the Supreme Council relieved Bayoomi of his task of forming an interim government and his position as premier-designate. It had always been a long-shot. The NLF and FLOSY had both threatened death to anyone who joined a Bayoomi government. Sir Humphrey knew that Bayoomi was not the best man for the job and that his prospective ministers were not of high calibre, but he had hoped to change the image of the federal government and so ease the way for a United Nations' mission to secure the collaboration of FLOSY and the NLF. The federal ministers' rejection of Bayoomi completed his disillusionment, and on his return from New York he warned them bluntly that they had no future in South Arabia on their own.

Sir Humphrey's journey to New York had the additional advantage that Mackawee was already there and in surreptitious touch with the UN mission. There was further encouragement on July 25, when the NLF announced that it would discuss South Arabia with members of the mission at any place they chose. In three days of close discussion with Pérez-Guerrero, Shelizi and M. L. Keita, Sir Humphrey finally dispelled the belief that Britain would sabotage all efforts to reach a settlement. He not only made the position clearer to the three members of the mission, but also convinced them that he sincerely wanted their help in bringing the NLF and FLOSY into collaboration. The three men undertook to renew their mission and set off for Geneva to hear evidence.

This was the last positive initiative to give even faint hope of a broadly based government. The High Commissioner had pulled all the stops and had hardly got a squeak out of any of them. The federal ministers had let him down. The NLF leaders withdrew their agreement to see the mission once they saw that FLOSY was getting nothing out of it. Six federal ministers, with whom the mission had refused to talk in the spring, met it in dreary conversation in Geneva while their states collapsed behind them in South Arabia. The mission went to Beirut to see the South Arabian League and to Cairo to talk to FLOSY; even then the NLF would have no part in the discussions. By that time, in any case, it was too late.

IV

British troops withdrew from the tribal hinterland in June. As they had no obligation to intervene outside Aden, they would return only if the federal government requested them to do so and the High Commissioner thought it justified. An attempt was made by FLOSY to take over by attacking from Yemen, but it failed to make headway against the federal army and the NLF. The NLF, indeed, was clearly well-established in all the main towns and was meeting little if any opposition from the army. By the end of August, its red, white, and black flag was flying over the village of Dar Saad, only ten miles from Aden across the Lahej border, and its supporters were in control of twelve of the states, including Lahej, Lower Yafa and Fadhli, the three most prosperous sultanates, and the Alawi, Aqrabi, Dhala, Lower Aulaqi, Upper Aulaqi and Wahidi territories.

The Federation was rapidly collapsing. On August 26, Sheikh Ali Musaid al-Bubakri, acting chairman of the Supreme Council and one of the only three ministers in Al-Ittihad, asked the army to take over power in the state. The High Command refused, for the very good reason that its forces were now tolerating or actively supporting the NLF, and Sheikh Ali resigned from the government. As though to underline the total disintegration, the tough old Sharif of Beihan departed of his own accord across the desert from his northern frontier state towards Riyadh, the Saudi capital. The NLF claimed the state two weeks later. At the beginning of September, the federal army asked Sir Humphrey Trevelyan to negotiate with the NLF and FLOSY. In fact, there was nothing left to do, for the tribal rulers had succumbed without a fight. He flew to London on September 3 to consult his government, and two days later returned to Aden to announce that, the federal government being defunct, he was ready to negotiate with the nationalist forces.

It was the end of an affair, of which nothing remained except a fair or foul farewell. Even this lay outside the power of British choice. If no one came to the wake, Britain could do no more than play itself out with a wild lament and slam the door on the corpse.

There was, however, a postscript to it all. The Eastern Protectorates—the Qaiti, Kathiri and Mahra sultanates whose membership of the Federation had seemed vital to Sir Charles Johnston—had never quite been forgotten. In his statement to the Commons of June 20, George Brown admitted that it was 'unlikely that they would commit themselves before independence'. (The only ground for thinking that they might ever join rested on the fact that the new nineteen-year-old Sultan of Qaiti, Ghalib bin Awadh, had tinkered with the idea the previous March.) The Foreign Secretary reminded the House that the Hadraumi Bedouin Legion was paid for and controlled by the British, and that when the British withdrew from South Arabia there would be nothing to prevent disorder in the three states. The British government would therefore pay for the legion for two years after the withdrawal if the three states worked out satisfactory command arrangements. On August 10, the three rulers announced that they had agreed to put it under joint command. In October, the NLF took over the whole Eastern region, and the Qaiti and Kathiri sultans took refuge in South Arabia.

Birth of the Republic

As the South Arabian Federation moved steadily to its death, the Yemen Republic struggled with mounting political and economic problems. As in Aden, civil war destroyed the natural economy of the country, so that the export of coffee, the country's main crop, had tumbled from its pre-revolutionary average of 35,000 tons a year to 5,000. A decision of the Federation to close the frontier added to the trading troubles. There was a shortage of food, and the government's coffers were so bare that, in order to pay its officials, it coerced Yemeni merchants into granting loans that would never be recovered. Prices were greatly inflated by the amount of paper money poured into the country from Egypt to pay for the Egyptian forces. One of Amri's quarrels with Nasser was his demand that Egypt should transfer foreign exchange to pay for the troops at a time when it had no foreign exchange to spare. The situation was only slightly eased when Nasser withdrew about one-third of his 70,000 army after concentrating them on the central plateau.

At the same time, there were many visible signs of post-revolution progress: more schools, piped water, more hospitals and clinics, and a large textile mill built by the Communist Chinese where, for the first time in Yemen's long history, women were working alongside men indoors. But all this was done with foreign money, mostly from Eastern Europe but also from the United States.

The disrupted tribal economy of the royalist areas was, if anything, in a worse plight than that of the republicans, for Saudi Arabian money could not maintain supplies of food over long mountain tracks by mule and camel. The country was tired of it all: of civil war, and of Egyptians and republicans, of royalists and the Imam's family, and the Saudi Arabians—all of whom were preventing the tribes from coming to terms in traditional fashion among themselves.

I

The military stalemate continued. Prince Abdullah bin Hassan, commander of the Howlan region of the royalist front and son of the royalist Prime Minister, Prince Hassan bin Yahya, was operating from his headquarters in a cave fifteen miles from Sanaa, unable to advance and yet safe from the nearby Egyptians. The royalist command, however, was being disrupted by the republican 'third force' and other dissidents who were proposing a pact by which they might jointly get rid of the Egyptians. As this greatly appealed to the Saudi government, which believed that, once the Egyptian army was out, its money could remove any danger to Saudi Arabia from Yemen, it was encouraging the plan and persuaded some of the royalist leaders, including Mohammed bin Hussein, the chief military leader and effectively deputy Imam, to agree to a coordinating committee which would organise a plebiscite when the Egyptians withdrew. The royalist Prime Minister and Imam Mohammed al-Badr would not commit themselves because Prince Abdullah bin Hassan was sulking about it in his Howlan cave and threatening to lay down his arms.

King Feisal was now feeling more confident. In April 1967, the first stage was completed of the Anglo-American air-defence system, costing more than £100 million. At Khamis Mushayt, fifty miles from the Yemeni frontier, the British had installed Thunderbird missile batteries, an early-warning radar system, and an airstrip where some Hawker-Hunter fighters flown by ex-RAF pilots were at the ready. The Americans had installed Hawk ground-to-ground anti-tank missiles at the Saudi port of Jizan even closer to the frontier, with radar that could reach Sanaa. Thunderbirds were being installed at Najran, which had once been attacked by Egyptian light bombers.

It was the Arab-Israeli war that changed the whole situation. At its outset, President Nasser told Sallal he must withdraw some of his troops and that Yemen would somehow have to pay for those that remained. The crushing defeat of Egypt, with the loss of most of its air force and ground artillery and tanks, made a reversal of this decision impossible. When Nasser took stock of the economic disaster, the loss of Sinai oil, the Suez Canal income and the tourist trade, he turned to the rich oil states for support. At the Arab summit conference at Khartoum in August 1967, Saudi Arabia, Libya and Kuwait agreed among them to provide £135 million a year for Egypt and Jordan, of which Egypt would get £95 million. Without waiting for Feisal's request, Nasser proposed a reactivation of the Jeddah agreement and a committee was set up—consisting of the Sudanese Prime Minister, Mohammed Mahgoub, and representatives of Morocco and Iraq—to see to its implementation and arrange for a political settlement in Yemen.

This time there could be no doubt about the Egyptian withdrawal. So, as the British were packing their bags in Aden, Nasser's troops were doing likewise in Yemen. The Sallal regime was doomed; and before the end of the year, while its President was in Baghdad on his way to Moscow, Qadi Abdel Rahman Iryani led the 'third force' in a bloodless coup in Sanaa.

II

The final withdrawal of the British forces from Aden began on August 25, 1967, when the first battalion of the South Wales Borderers began to leave for home and were not replaced by equivalent infantry troops. They had patrolled the troublesome Maala district since January and in the course of 350 incidents had killed eleven, wounded ten and captured eighteen. Royal Marines moved in for the time being. The South Arabian Army and the High Commission announced a timetable for the withdrawal of 12,000 British troops, to be completed by January 9, 1968.

Sir Humphrey Trevelyan's appeal on September 5 to the militants to come forward met with no response. Instead, PORF, for FLOSY, and the NLF began to fight each other in Sheikh Othman, Mansoura and the village of Dar Saad just across the border in Lahej. Dar Saad was the scene of the worst fighting, and at least twenty men on each side were killed and hundreds wounded. The struggle for power was now in the open. Each party was trying to establish its ascendancy over the other, and each sought to utilise contacts with the British or the UN mission solely to help it along the road. Because the British now clearly recognised the dominant position of the NLF upcountry and in the army, Qahtan as-Shaabi was willing to talk with them on condition that the discussion would be concerned only with the ways and means for the NLF's taking power. On September 2, he met pressmen (for the first time in South Arabia since 1963), at Zinjibar, capital of the Fadhli state, where, surrounded by about 300 of his heavily armed commandos and apparently on excellent terms with the federal army, he laid down his terms.

The British were not yet ready to rule out FLOSY or to impose NLF power. For its part, FLOSY was withering away, although it still had minority support in the army; about seventy of its PORF fighters deserted to the NLF. In these circumstances, it agreed to talk to the UN mission which, totally ignorant of the true situation, still accepted the Cairo view that FLOSY was the main party in South Arabia.

There were still some neutral high officers among the top brass of the South Arabian Army. Sir Humphrey Trevelyan, aided by its British commander, Brigadier Jack Dye, persuaded them at last that there was no future in civil war between the parties. On September 7, they ordered the rivals to stop fighting and decide whether they were willing to talk with Sir Humphrey about implementing the UN resolutions. The Arab League also called all parties in South Arabia—including the federal rulers, the South Arabian League and Bayoomi's United National Party—to a conference in Cairo. The League was either behind the times or desired to outweigh the influence of the NLF. Whatever the reason, Qahtan as-Shaabi indignantly refused to discuss anything with the 'stooges'. He did, however, respond to the appeal of the army by agreeing to talk with

FLOSY; but it was evident that he intended a subordinate role for his rivals. The immediate outcome of the army's intervention was a cease-fire between the two groups of militants.

The army leaders continued their efforts to get the two together, but the NLF, seeking to demonstrate its total control of South Arabia, wanted the conference to take place on its own territory, whereas FLOSY desired to meet in Cairo under the mediation of Nasser. The army sought a compromise by suggesting a meeting in Beirut, Khartoum or Asmara. The NLF at last gave way and, on October 7, Qahtan as-Shaabi and his cousin Feisal arrived in Cairo at the head of his delegation. Sir Humphrey Trevelyan waited in Aden for their joint approach and meanwhile busied himself and the British army commanders with the final programme for evacuation and the security of the British civilian population.

This was still an important question. On September 25, the British troops had pulled out of the two worst trouble spots, Mansoura and Sheikh Othman, and handed them over to the South Arabian Army. With Crater firmly in the hands of the Argyll and Sutherland Highlanders and no obvious British targets in Mansoura or Sheikh Othman, the nationalist assassins moved down to Steamer Point. The British left the Arab quarter to them and covered the port, the hotels and the road to Tarshyne, where the High Commission and the army commanders worked inside a wired and guarded area. Any Englishman who strayed outside this control line was killed.

After negotiating for nearly a month in Cairo, FLOSY and the NLF announced on November 1 that they had reached agreement and that the names of a joint delegation to negotiate with the British would be announced soon. The object of British policy was now to get out of Aden as quickly as possible, for the troops held only Crater, the port area and the Khormaksar airport and military camps. On the following day, therefore, George Brown told the House of Commons that the July plan for a settlement would have to be 'altered'. British troops would complete their evacuation in the last half of November; moreover, as Egypt was evacuating Yemen, there was no longer any need to provide naval forces and

V-bombers to protect South Arabia after independence. Recalling that Britain had promised financial support to the defunct Federation, the Foreign Secretary said that judgement on this should be suspended until the attitude of the new government was known. His efforts to internationalise Perim, at the gateway to the Red Sea, had failed and the island would stay as part of South Arabia.

This straightforward declaration precipitated the final struggle for power between FLOSY and NLF in Aden and the complete abandonment of the Cairo agreement. Within twenty-four hours, about 3,500 NLF 'commandos' were locked in battle with 500 heavily armed FLOSY men all over Aden. In the course of four days, and despite the efforts of the South Arabian Army, more than 100 Arabs were killed and 300 wounded. In the end, it became clear that the army was on the side of the NLF. At one stage, its Saladin armoured car silenced FLOSY guns; and, when the fighting at last stopped, the army had 700 FLOSY men in custody. The NLF had about 1,250 in detention, including some police, FLOSY army officers and 250 Yemeni royalists. Although FLOSY leaders in Cairo promised to continue the battle for supremacy, their people in Aden and South Arabia were in hiding or on the run. On November 7, George Brown admitted to the Commons that the NLF had won, and that day the High Command of the South Arabian Army announced that the NLF controlled the entire country, had the support of 95 per cent of the people, and 'had the right to speak for the people in their hour of destiny'.

Saif Ahmed al-Dhalai, chairman of the NLF's political committee, sent a message to Brown through the High Commissioner, calling on him to name a delegation; and on November 14, the Foreign Secretary announced that Lord Shackleton would lead the British team for talks in Geneva beginning on November 21. He added that British troops would complete their withdrawal by November 30, on which day South Arabia would become independent.

Qahtan as-Shaabi led the NLF delegation, which consisted of Dhalai, Feisal as-Shaabi, Mohammed Ahmed al-Bechbechi, Abdul Fattah Ismail and nine advisers, including Major Salem al-Menahi of the Hadraumi Bedouin Legion of the Eastern Protectorate area which was never part of the Federation. During the Geneva talks, Qahtan stated that the name of the new state would be the People's Republic of South Yemen. In the early hours of November 29, after an all-night session, agreement was reached whereby all Britain's rights were to be vested in the republic. It was agreed that the two countries would establish diplomatic relations and continue the discussion of outstanding problems through their respective missions.

The most important question concerned the amount of aid Britain would give the republic. Dhalai and others had frequently stated that the new government had the right to receive assistance totalling £60 million over three years, which was the amount promised to the Federation. There were manifest difficulties in the way of this. It could hardly be a worse period to discuss the matter because the financial plight of Britain had just forced devaluation of sterling; moreover, the money had been promised to a government likely to be friendly to Britain, whereas there was no reason to assume good relations with the republic, and the sentiment of the British people was against giving large sums to people who had been killing British soldiers and civilians until only a few days earlier. Lord Shackleton was, however, able to promise the NLF £3 million already in the coffers in Aden and a further £12 million. These gifts were not announced; it was simply stated that the matter of 'further' aid would be discussed later.

On the morning of November 28, Sir Humphrey Trevelyan's personal flag was lowered and he flew off to Bahrein and London. In a brief message on parting he wished the new state a happy and prosperous future and hoped for good relations between it and Britain. On the following day, the last British unit was lifted by helicopter to the waiting warships, and at midnight November 29–30, 1967, the People's Republic of South Yemen was born. Qahtan as-Shaabi and his team, who had had an aircraft standing by at Geneva, arrived in time for the dramatic moment. He was proclaimed President and took up residence in the former High Commissioner's house on Tarshyne Point.

It had been a long and painful birth. Since the emergency regulations were enforced on December 10, 1963, 398 people had been killed and 1,814 wounded in Aden. Two-thirds of the casualties were local Arabs and almost all the rest were British soldiers or civilians. The British forces had also lost 57 killed and 235 wounded elsewhere in South Arabia, but the Arab casualties upcountry were unknown. The final stages of the evacuation took place without incident, although thousands of Adenis celebrated continuously from November 26, when the British troops pulled out of Crater, Maala and Tawahi, and Brigadier Jack Dye, the British commander of the South Arabia Army, relinquished his post to Mohammed Ahmed al-Aulaqi.

On December 1, President Qahtan as-Shaabi addressed a cheering mass of people at Al-Ittihad, which had been renamed the People's City, stating that the policy of the government would be socialism at home, non-alignment abroad, Arab unity, the liberation of Palestine, support for national revolutionary movements and the 'reunification of the Arab people in north and south Yemen'. He also gave the names of his first government, in which he would be Prime Minister and Supreme Commander of the Armed Forces.*

Apart from the president, who was forty-seven, they were all young men in their thirties and hardly known in South Arabia, let alone outside it. This was partly due to their working 'underground' in the NLF for almost four years. They were all men of some education and most of them with training in government service under the British, and when they emerged it became clear that they had made a very thorough study of both the military and political aspects of revolution all the way from Marx and Lenin to Castro and Mao Tse-tung. They were for the most part Arab Socialists of the Nasser type rather than Communists, except, perhaps the Minister of National Guidance, Abdul Fattah Ismail, who was reputed to be a Marxist. It was evident at the Geneva conference

---

Foreign Affairs, Saif Ahmed al-Dhalai; *Defence*, Ali Salem al-Baidh; *Interior and Acting Health Minister*, Mohammed Ali Haithem; *Finance*, Mahmoud Abdullah Oshaish; *Culture, National Guidance and Yemen Unity Affairs*, Abdul Fattah Ismail al-Jaufi; *Economy, Commerce, Planning*, Feisal Abdul Latif as-Shaabi; *Justice, Waqfs* (religious endowments), Abdel Mahfoudh Khalifa; *Works and Communications*, Faisal Shamlan; *Labour and Welfare*, Abdul Malik Ismail; *Education*, Mohammed Abdul Kader Bafiqih; *Local Government and Agriculture*, Seyyid Omar Akbar.

that they had prepared very carefully for the moment when they would take power. They were well-documented on all the issues and greatly surprised the British delegates, who expected them to be revolutionary fighters rather than politicians, by their grasp of the issues at stake. Lord Shackleton himself thought they were men of high calibre. Dhalai, who had emerged from obscurity in the few weeks immediately preceding independence as the director of the political bureau based on Zinjibar, made a similar impression on journalists who went out there to see him.

President Qahtan as-Shaabi was the only well-known man in the leadership, his career having been traced through the South Arabian League to the foundation of the NLF and afterwards. He was a small chubby man whose appearance belied his revolutionary nature until the dramatic gestures accompanying his fanatic speech gave evidence of his inner passion. He was born in Lahej in 1920. After passing through Aden College, he graduated as an agricultural engineer at Khartoum University and returned to Lahej as an agricultural officer. He formed the nucleus of his movement from the young members of a literary society in Sheikh Othman but in 1958 he chose voluntary exile in Cairo in order to oppose the Federation. In 1962, he went to Yemen to help the revolution and for a time was a minister in the republican government. He returned to Aden in 1963 to organise the NLF on the pattern of the Algerian FLN which had successfully overcome the French. Throughout his career he made no secret of the fact that he was a convinced Socialist and an implacable enemy of the British.

III

The problems facing the new government were immense. The economy was in ruins. Years of disorders had brought trade in Aden almost to a standstill, with only some of the entrepôt trade from Africa and Asia to sustain it. The biggest firm of all, A. B. Besse and Company, was run down to its hard core, which was all that remained between it and closing down; only the young principal, M. Antone Besse, and his general manager were standing by in the hope of better times ahead. Many of the Indians who had been running small firms had retreated to their home country. The thriving retail trade of the free port was at a standstill because few ships came into Aden, and the crews and passengers of those that did were afraid to come ashore. The BP refinery was doing some extra work for the Egyptian government because the Israelis had destroyed the Suez refineries, but there was little prospect of its getting back to normal because the Suez Canal was still closed and there was no sign of an early reopening. For the same reason, the port, which was the main source of Aden's revenue, was almost idle. The £11 million annual income from the British base was gone forever. The restoration of peace in Aden would clearly lead to some improvement, but, since Aden was almost the only source of revenue, the economy of the new republic was bound to stay depressed as long as the Suez Canal remained closed.

The tribal areas depended for enrichment on the development of agriculture, but no major improvement could be effected without the expenditure of very large sums of money over a long period of time on irrigation. The new government favoured land reform, which could make for better distribution among more people of such wealth as the state produced, but this would not increase wealth and, indeed, might, as Egypt discovered, reduce it for a time. A lot depended on how much foreign aid the republic obtained from abroad and how quickly. The financial assistance provided by Britain was required in its entirety for the army and the administration, and would not last a year.

The problem of security was immense in Aden and upcountry, for there were weapons and explosives everywhere. The leaders of FLOSY had sworn to maintain the struggle, and insurgency would certainly emerge again if discontent with the government manifested itself or there was a split in its ranks. The form of protest would be by armed struggle because tolerance of political dissent was unknown to the country. In the tribal areas, the NLF had been successful in taking over the population centres, but it remained doubtful whether the tribesmen either understood or wished for the kind of socialism that the new government stood for. It was therefore by no means certain that the apparent unity of the country would endure for long.

How well the government or its successors could survive the early difficulties depended to a large extent on the South Yemen Army which by this time stood at 8½ battalions. The British had aimed to make it ten battalions, but achievement of this strength depended on the money available from Britain. The army had acquitted itself well after it recovered from the June 20 mutiny, and with the FLOSY men removed from its ranks, it looked as though it could take care of the internal security of the state for some time to come.

The over-all picture was not promising, and certainly not what Britain had hoped for when it embarked on the road to independence in South Arabia. Yet, in the sense that one primary problem had been removed by the defeat of the tribal rulers, the end-result was probably a more realistic one than anything that could have been achieved by bringing them into alliance with the Adeni politicians. Britain's fault lay in trying to make a logical pattern in an area that totally lacked it. This misjudgement may well have been due to the mixed motives that went to the making of British policy: the desire of people on the spot to improve the lot of the people in the tribal areas and, on the other hand, the desire to keep Aden and the military base secure. To a large extent, Britain drifted into this policy when it entered into the advisory treaties. Although Harold Ingrams, the initiator of the advisory system, certainly never intended it, Britain became more and more involved in the running of the tribal areas.

History may well record that in this lay the fundamental error, since Britain had no real interest at stake in the Protectorate states beyond ensuring the security of Aden port. Britain and the tribes had lived happily together in South Arabia for about a century when each tried not to notice the other's existence more than necessary; and with a certain amount of modest help, such as the Abyan and Lahej cotton developments, they might have continued to do so until Britain bowed gracefully out of Aden. Political pressures would certainly have emerged and radically changed the area in time, but the probability of a peaceful transformation after

Britain departed would have been high but for the deep involvement of British policy in the tribal states.

It was the federal plan that generated the belief that Britain was imposing a reactionary regime and drove Qahtan as-Shaabi and his associates into open rebellion. As the records of all the negotiations to secure Aden's merger proved, no one in the Colony, not even the moderates who were working with the British, wanted rule by the sultans. The support for Britain therefore withered away, and it vanished entirely when the decision to make a total withdrawal was announced in London. This left Britain with only the federal government to work with, a government essentially of tribal rulers, since the Adeni federal ministers represented only a small minority of the Colony's population.

This was far from the desired result, and Sir Humphrey Trevelyan did his utmost to change it. By this time it was too late because the struggle for power, which had been at the root of the situation from the outset, was beyond control. The sultans were using the British to impose their rule; Asnaj and the People's Socialist Party tried to break into the government when the Labour Party came to power in Britain and, failing to do so, went over to open resistance with Egyptian backing. In doing so, it was animated largely by the belief that the NLF was gaining ground by armed struggle, also with Egyptian support. Each was seeking to dominate the country when the British left, and when the sultans were overthrown it became a straight fight between the two militant parties. From the moment Sir Humphrey became High Commissioner in May 1967, the bloodshed could be explained only by the intention of each militant leadership to destroy the other.

Undoubtedly, the presence of a large Egyptian army in Yemen contributed to the trouble. Both sets of militants were encouraged by the propaganda support, training and arms they got from Taiz. The British and the sultans were governed in almost every act by the fear that the Egyptian army would, on one pretext or another, invade from Yemen. Whether there was ever real justification for this fear will now never be known, but Sir Richard Turnbull publicly discounted it when he was High Commissioner and it is at least a reasonable assumption that Nasser never sought to do more than secure a government sympathetic to his policies in South Arabia. At any rate, as early as the summer of 1963, there were good grounds for supposing that his military involvement in Yemen was proving so difficult and damaging that he would be unlikely to extend it southwards.

The outcome was a country broken by conflict. The People's Republic of South Yemen had a government fairly well to Egypt's liking. The security of Aden, which had been the main object of the federal exercise in the first place, was beyond British influence except for the tenuous hold that financial aid might sustain for a time.

It yet remains to be seen whether the financial difficulties of the new republic will restrain its revolutionary fervour. Its leaders have for long been hostile to the Saudi Arabian government and the Yemeni royalists and dedicated, in the manner of Arab revolutionary socialists, to the overthrow of all traditional rulers in the Arab world. They will certainly desire to encourage the overthrow of the Sultan of Muscat and Oman, whose territories could become an extension of their own and have the great attraction of new oilfields, and they can also be expected to foster rebellion in the Persian Gulf. Since both these areas are of interest to Britain, from which the Republic of South Yemen requires certainly not less than the £60 million originally promised to the Federation, the republican leaders will need to consider carefully how far they will push their revolutionary purpose at the expense of their country's economy. They may well be counting on support from the Soviet bloc, believing that Russia will be ready to pay heavily for the disturbance of an area where Britain and the United States have great oil interests at stake.

There is nothing in their past to suggest that they will be captive to the policies of Egypt or any other Arab state, for they came to power along their own independent course, refusing to be the satellite of Egypt even when they most required its arms and ammunition for the continuation of their 'war of liberation'. They will speak loudly in favour of revolutionary policies, but their acts may be coloured by their need to live cautiously in a land where neither security nor money is easily come by.

Short Bibliography

Barbour, Nevill, "Aden and the Arab South", *The World Today*, London August 8, 1959.

Condé, Bruce, "The Federation of Arab Emirates of the South", *Middle East Forum*, Beirut, No. 8, October 1959.

Hickinbotham, Sir Tom, *Aden*, Constable, London 1958.

Holden, David, *Farewell to Arabia*, Faber, London 1966; Walker, New York 1966.

Ingrams, Harold, *Arabia and the Isles*, Murray, London 1966; Praeger, New York 1966.

Johnston, Sir Charles H., *The View from Steamer Point*, Collins, London 1964; Praeger, New York 1964.

Kilner, Peter, "The Future of South Arabia", April 1965; "Britain, the UN and South Arabia", August 1966; "South Arabian Independence", August 1967: all articles in *The World Today*, London.

King, Gillian, *Imperial Outpost—Aden*, Royal Institute of International Affairs, London 1964.

Little, Tom, *Modern Egypt*, Benn, London 1967; Praeger, New York 1967.

Lunt, James, *The Barren Rocks of Aden*, Herbert Jenkins, London 1966.

Reilly, Sir Bernard, *Aden and the Yemen*, HMSO, London 1960.

Ronart, Stephen and Ronart, Nandy, *Concise Encyclopaedia of Arabic Civilisation*, Vol. I, *The Arab East*, Djambatan, Amsterdam 1959; Praeger, New York 1960.

Stark, Freya, *The Southern Gates of Arabia*, Murray, London 1936.

South Arabia was reported continuously in the British press (and, to a lesser extent, in the American press) from 1962 onwards, and therefore newspaper files in libraries provide a unique and valuable source of reference. *The Mideast Mirror*, published weekly by Regional News Services (Mid-East) Ltd., Beirut, has also given a reliable account of the region since 1949.

Index

Abbasids, 7, 11
Abdali tribes, 6, 11–12, 130
Abdel Aziz ibn Saud: see Saud
Abdel Kerim, Sultan (c. 1918), 15
Abdel Kerim, Sultan Ahmed ibn, (c. 1802), 10, 11
Abdel Kerim, Sultan Ali (c. 1952), 14, 50, 56–8, 70, 89, 140
Abdullah, Ahmed, Sultan of Fadhli, 112–13
Abdullah, Prince Seif al-Islam, 38–9, 47–9, 93
Abdullah bin Hassan, Prince, 175
Abdullah bin Uthman, 59n
Abdullah ibn Ziyad, 11
Abu Arish, 8
Abu Bakr, Caliph, 6, 7
Abu Dhabi, 48
Abyan Development Board, 52–3, 127–9, 184
Abyssinia (Ethiopia), 4, 5, 23, 83
Aden, passim; becomes Colony, 17–18; British impose direct rule on, 142–3, 146; Constitutions for, 62–4, 68, 78, 152–4, 169; description of, 120–2; early history, 5–6, 8–9, 11; effects of Yemeni revolution on, 94–5; importance as British base, 14, 77, 79, 81, 84, 88, 95–6, 101–2, 104, 112, 120–3; merger with Protectorates, 68–88, 94–117, 147; population and nationalities, 122–4, 185; security plans for, 168–9, 183; social welfare, 122–5; State of Emergency in, 103–4, 114, 141–3, 161; terrorism in, 150, 157–8, 162–3, 168–9; trade, 83, 183; union with Federation, 108; UN missions in, q.v.; withdrawal of troops from, 148–9, 159,

171, 176, 178–81 (See also British in Aden)
Aden Association, 32–3, 64, 69–70
Aden College, 124, 129–30, 182
Aden Protectorates: advisory treaties with, 29–31, 184; constituents of, 16n.; Federation plan proposed, 42–5; Levies, 21, 26, 28, 49, 52, 57, 71; organisation of states, 130–1
Aden Settlement, 15–17
Aden TUC: see Trade Union Congress
Afghanistan, 162
Agriculture, 126–7, 129, 183
Ahl Nakhai tribe, 52
Ahmed, Alawi, 27
Ahmed, Seif al-Islam, Imam of Yemen, 37–41, 88–90, 94, 133; attempt on life, 92; death of, 93; first press conference, 51; opposes federal plan, 45–51, 58; relations with Nasser, 54–6, 90–1; Russian association, 61; sends al-Badr to London, 52
Ahmed am-Mohsin, 27
Ahmed bin Abdullah, Naib of Fadhli, 42n., 56, 59, 140
Ahmed ibn Muhasin, Sultan (1847), 14
Airport grenade outrage, 103, 115
Akbar, Seyyid Omar, 181n.
Al-Ahmar, Abdullah bin Hussein, 133
Al-Ahram, 145
Al-Amoudi, Salem, 164
Al-Amri, Hassan, 144–5, 155, 174
Al-Asnaj, Abdullah, 80, 85, 98, 101, 112–14, 117–19, 139–42, 146–7, 151–2, 155, 165, 185
Al-Audhali, Sultan Saleh, 153
Al-Aulaqi, Mohammed Ahmed, 180

Index

Hashid tribes, 89–90, 133
Hassan, Prince (brother of Ahmed), 92–3
Hassan bin Yahya, Prince, 175
Haushabi sultans, 10, 44, 59n., 108
Healey, Dennis, 114, 141
Health services, 42, 83, 124–5, 128
Hedjaz, 19, 23, 110
Henderson, George, 103–4, 112
Hickinbotham, Sir Tom, 27, 31, 42, 44–6, 50, 59–60, 64
Himyarites, 4–6, 9, 11–12
Hobson, Laurence, 88
Hodeida, 8, 18–20, 51, 89–90, 92, 134
Holden, David, 69, 149
Hone, Sir Ralph, 142
Hone-Bell constitution, 152–4, 169
Hospitals, 92, 124–5, 128, 174
Howlan region, 175
Humaidi tribe, 57
Husn al-Ghurab island, 3
Hussein, King of Jordan, 61
Hussein, Sharif of Beihan, 8, 56
Husseini, Mohammed, 81–4, 97, 104

Ibb: bomb incident at, 92
Ibrahim Pasha, 8
Idrisi Arabs, 18
Incense Route, 2–3, 9
India: trade with, 2–4
Indians in Aden, 17, 32, 48, 63, 73, 102, 123–4, 149, 183
Indonesia, 23
Industrial Court, 67
Industrial Relations Ordinance (1960), 67, 100
Infantry Brigade, 24th, 105
Ingrams, Harold, 22, 24–6, 29
International Commission of Jurists, 156
Iraq, 37, 77, 101, 176; murder of royal family, 61; revolution celebrations, 91
Iryani, Qadi Abdel Rahman, 144–5, 155, 176
Ismail, Abdul Fattah: see Al-Jaufi
Ismail, Abdul Malik, 181n.

Israel, 6, 168, 176
Italy, 19

Jaar, 131
Jabal al-Ras, 7
Jabal Jihaf, 57
Jabal Manawa: fort at, 38
Jacob, Lieutenant-Colonel, 19
Jeddah agreement, 143, 145, 149, 157, 176
Jerusalem, 3; fall of, 5, 6, 123
Jews in South Arabia, 4–6, 123–4
Jifri, Abdullah, 56, 117, 152
Jifri, Alawi, 56, 117, 152
Jifri, Mohammed Ali, 50, 55–7, 70, 117, 147, 152
Jihaf, Mt., 57
Jihafi tribe, 57
Jizan, 175
Johnston, Sir Charles, 66–7, 74, 79n., 85, 95, 102n., 105, 109, 173
Jordan, 2, 61, 93, 106, 176
Joshi, V. K., 80

Kamaran island, 17–19, 50, 52
Kasim, Abdel Rahim, 164
Kathiri desert, 23
Kathiri sultanate, 23–4, 26, 29, 45, 108–10, 113, 139, 173
Keita, Moussa Leo, 162, 171
Keith Falconer Medical Mission, 20
Kenya, 61, 105
Kerim: see Abdel Kerim
Khalifa, Abdel Mahfoudh, 181n.
Khamis Mushayt, 175
Kharibah, 3
Khartoum, 117, 176, 178
Kholan tribes, 133
Khormaksar, 121, 125, 178
Khrushchev, Nikita S., 61
Koadel, Abu Bakr, 99
Kuria Muria islands, 17
Kuwait, 77, 140, 156, 176
Kuwatly, President Shukry, 53

Lahej, state and sultans of, 10–15, 29, 32, 44, 49–50, 53, 55–9, 70, 72,

Index

Index

Trades Union Congress (UK), 67, 118

Trevaskis, G. K. N. (later Sir Kennedy), 42, 75, 101-4, 107-10, 112, 114-16

Trevelyan, Sir Humphrey, 166-73, 176-80, 185

Tribal Guards, 21, 28, 51-3

Tribes: *see under* South Arabia

Tunisia, 140

Turks, 7-10, 12-15, 18-19

Turnbull, Sir Richard, 116, 161, 164-6, 186

Tyre, 3

United Arab Republic, 53-5, 61, 64, 140 (*See also* Egypt)

United National Front, 32-3, 50, 70

United National Party, 80, 86, 99, 158n., 177

United Nations, 37-9, 47, 136-7, 153-4, 157, 159-60; missions to Aden, 162-5, 171, 177; proposals for South Arabian government, 167; Special Committee on Colonialism, 102-3

United States of America, 37, 51, 89, 95, 111, 175, 186

U Thant, 136, 157, 163

Uthman: *see* Abdullah bin

Venezuela: delegation from, 162

'Violet Line', 40

Van Horn, General Carl, 136

Wadi Bana, 129

Wadi Beihan, 38

Wadi Hadramaut, 23, 109

Wadi Harib, 38

Wadi, Marqad, 38

Wadi Saba (Wadi al-Sadd), 3

Wadi Tiban, 127

Wahabis, 7-8, 12

Wahidis, 23, 45, 108, 172

Western Protectorate, 15, 16n., 21, 29n., 30, 66, 103, 107, 115; federation scheme, 43-5, 56, 58-60; states in, 108-10

Wilson, Harold, 114, 165

Wilton, John, 170

Yafai tribes and sultanates, 5-6, 10, 15, 24, 29n., 52-3, 59, 108, 127, 132, 172; agricultural scheme, 129-30; education, 130

Yahya, Imam, 12, 18-20, 36-7, 92

Yahya ibn Hussein al-Rassi, Imam (*c.* 897), 7

Yemen, *passim*; Anglo-US defences for, 175; association with UAR, 54-5, 63-4, 91; boundary dispute with British, 38-9; civil war in, 93-5, 108, 117, 134, 156; description of, 132; education, 133, 174; Egyptian troops in, *see under* Egypt; famine (1959), 89; Imams of, 7, 12-15, 20n., 72-3, 132-3 (*see also* Ahmed); Nine Cantons, 15; opposes settlement with Britain, 140; republic, beginnings of, 88, 174-86; Sallal's government (1966), 155-6; system of government, 133-4; tribes, *see under* South Arabia; UN mission received, 102; Yemeni community in Aden, 63, 72, 94

Yemen Development Corporation, 37

Yemen Progressive Union, 135

Yugoslavia, 52

Zabid, 8

Zanzibar, 22-3

Zaphar, 4

Zeidis, 7-8, 12, 18, 36n., 46, 56, 80, 133

Zinjibar, 131, 177, 182

Ziyadites, 11

Zubeiri, Sheikh Mohammed, 144